WHEN LOVE
IS NOT ENOUGH

HOW WILL I KNOW?

DR DIANE D CARTER

Printed in the United States of America

First paperback edition April 2022

ISBN 978-1-66784-307-0

ISBN 978-166784-308-7

This book in dedicated to a very special man in my life without whom this book would not have been written. We have come a long way together and I am proud to call you Elijah D. Carter, (EJ) my son.

FOREWORD

With each passing year, it becomes clearer to me that family is not only about "blood" or legal relationships. Family, in a single word, is about choice. This truth is most evident in the relationship between mother and child. A quote attributed to Oprah Winfrey is quite fitting – "Biology is the least of what makes someone a mother." The book you hold in your hands is not a fairytale; rather, it paints an honest and transparent picture of some of the unpleasant aspects of motherhood.

I first witnessed Diane's deep desire to be a parent shortly after my son was born – she doted on him as if she had given birth to him. Several years later, I was not the least bit surprised when she announced her intention to embark on the journey of adopting a child. Although I had my reservations concerning the wisdom of that choice, I respected and admired her willingness to follow her dream of becoming a mom. I often joke that God does not allow women (or men) to see into the future of their parenthood journeys because the human race would cease to exist. Some might wonder if Diane had foreseen the challenges, and indeed the intermittent nightmares, of choosing to adopt and parent a child through a public entity, whether she may have chosen a different route. Anyone who knows and loves her, as I do, does not believe for a moment that she would abandon that calling. Her tenacity and commitment to love her son unconditionally, to fight for him, and ultimately to make hard choices concerning him, are a testament to her strength of character, her spiritual walk with God and her resilience.

Although this book should serve as a cautionary tale for anyone considering adoption through a public organization, I hope that it also serves as an inspiration to anyone who dreams of being a parent. Whether you are a mother through birth or adoption, I encourage you to ask yourself what you will do when love is not enough to successfully raise your child.

SLN

PREFACE

The purpose of this book is to expose the corruption and dysfunction of a system whose goal is for the protection of CHILDREN. Unfortunately, I've found that the System often throws the baby out with the bath water in it's attempts at securing child protection. Many times, innocent parents are caught in the web of criminal law and order.

A system I depended on to provide guidance as I endeavor to adopt a child turned out to be very intimidating, unorganized in many aspects, non supportive and a nightmare. The havoc that was wreaked into my life can never be remedied or dissolved. I shall never forget the many nights of fear, terror and lonliness as I fought not only for my freedom and sanity but for a child, I've never birthed however a child that needed my love as much as I needed to provide it.

With the state of Georgia having one of the highest numbers of children in foster care, it becomes imperative to channel energies in to making both foster care and adoption palatable. It is my goal in this book to point out both mistakes I've made in my decision to adopt and how to avoid those that are preventable. Also, for those of you who are already parents and would never consider fostering or adoption, please do not think you are safe, and this book is not for you! The System knows no boundaries. Children in the system called the Department of Family and Children Services did not ask to be born and they need Love to pull them out of a system which uses them as a form of legal slavery.

The incidents documented are very true after all, this is a Non-Fiction book despite the names having been changed. This book is for adults who have children regardless of the children being special needs or not and for parents who have adopted or are fostering or are considering. This system had been around for ages therefore it is highly unlikely to be changed within itself, however, we as the adults / parents needed to provide the fuel which drives the engine, have the power to enforce certain righteous decisions on behalf of those who can not speak for themselves, OUR CHILDREN!

ACKNOWLEDGEMENT

The hardest part of writing this book is the acknowledgements. There are so many people who helped me in my journey of becoming a mom that it would be a mistake to try and list everyone. I truly got a revelation that "it takes a village to raise a child". So let me start by thanking God the Father, God the Son (Jesus) and God the Holy Spirit; without divine intervention I seriously doubt if I would still be here living in the goodness of the Lord. I also want to thank God for those special, anointed people (you know who you are), who have enriched and impacted my life. Thanks for the encouragement, guidance, and prayers. You will never fully realize how much I deeply appreciate your imput at just the right time. You were the "IT" factor that kept me going when I wanted to give up or give in. May you be richly blessed for all the kindness and wisdom shown to my son and me.

However, there is an elite category that demands honorable acknowledgements to the following: Dr. Creflo and Taffi Dollar, my pastors, and spiritual parents. Although I was not able to meet with them when I thought the need to, their constant flow of God's word to me, from the pulpit, online, books and ebooks and social media kept me spiritually strengthened and moving forward. Today, I continue to grow in my Godly relationship because of them reaching out beyond the traditional Sunday morning service, proof that one doesn't need to have a 1:1 "with the Pastor" to get what's needed, however, you do need to listen to the word going forth and apply it to your life, hence the importance of finding the right church home. I thank God for my church!

To Jeff Sparks, the brother God sent into my life; we were siblings in Christ long before my decision to adopt. You have been by my side before, during and after my adoption. You were at the signing of the papers making my adoption legal and you were at every CPS/DFCS court proceedings with me, and there were many. You even helped me get out of jail when my attorney failed me. My true brother in Christ, I love you and thank you for being an uncle and role model to my son, my anchor when I felt unsteady and the confirmation in the absence of feedback from a man's point of view.

To Serena Nowell, my sister in Christ and BFF, thank you for your support, prayers, patience, and the list goes on. I could always call on you no matter what time it was. Thank you for being that confidant when circumstances and situations were extremely sensitive. I never feared my business being misplaced with you. I love you and thank you for always having my back.

To my sister Terri, it was you I made my initial call to, when I had learned that there was a little boy waiting for me to adopt. We prayed together while I was driving to the office of DFCS to meet my new son. I'll never forget how weeks later; you used your experience as a mom to gradually introduce my son to the beach when I was about to freak out because he was freaking out at seeing so much sand and the ocean. LOL. We've always been close and although we became estranged in 2016, I thank God for reconciliation. Thank you for sharing your experiences with my son and me, all the fun trips with just the three of us and the continued love and laughter.

To Candee' Winfield, my Counselor; thanks for all the times you allowed me to cry when I needed to, vent and/or just be silent during my healing, and all without judgement. It was you who was instrumental in titling this book and I am forever grateful.

To Pam Kelly, my long-time sister friend who through the entire eight plus years of laboring over this book, you helped me with the manuscript, computer issues, Word application issues not to mention after I bought a new computer, there were new issues to deal with. Thanks so much for your patience, love, and expertise. I have no idea what I would have done without you Sis.

To my spiritual son, Pastor Anthony Adams at WCCI Teen Ministry, I had no idea that the little boy I embraced and called "my son", (even with your mom side eyeing me), would one day grow up and be the key person to help me with my adopted son, let alone become a Youth Pastor. You have no idea how much you impacted my son and unto this day, he remembers things that you shared with him from a man's point of view. At times, you and I had wondered if we were getting through, but you always told me, he's getting it and one day we'll see it, well, you were right. Thanks so much for your patience and wisdom at such a young age. I learned so much from you as well. I once told my son that you were my first son, as I remembered my many attempts keeping you out of trouble with your real mom when you were young. I love you "Ant".

To everyone at World Changers Church International Children's Ministry and Teen Ministry. You know who you are as my son, and I had many 1:1 sessions and fun times with you. Thank you so much for accepting my son for the way he was and helping him to metamorphis into the creation God has predestined him to be. I am so grateful for your acceptance of him in a world where he only knew rejection. I am teary eyed sitting here writing this as I think of the kindness shown us, especially in teen ministry where there were many new challenges and boundaries were being crossed. From his younger years in children's ministy to his older years in teen ministry, you all DEMONSTRATED God's word to him, it was so much more than just the spoken word. I am so proud to have been a fellow servant in Children's Ministry with you all for over twenty-five years. Blessings to ALL the volunteers!

CONTENTS

PROLOGUE

"For [the Spirit which] you have now received [is] not a spirit of slavery to put you once more in bondage to fear, but you have received the Spirit of adoption [the Spirit producing sonship] in [the bliss of] which we cry, Abba (Father)! Father!" (Romans 8:15 AMP)

It's a parent's worst nightmare. It comes suddenly, and at times it's unexpected. The intrusion, always unwanted, is to be compared with the residue from forced copulation. Many lives are affected by this invasion of privacy; however, the ones most affected are the innocents. One thinks, this will never happen to me yet, this invasion, intrusion, rape, is no respecter of people, race, or ethnic background. It functions just like its father, the Satan, in that it's very deceptive, cunning, and full of lies and perversion. It can cause the truth to be twisted like a piece of wicker. It brings confusion to innocent minds of children, and while it speaks of family unity, behind the scenes are forces at work to totally separate. It advertises foster care, for it loathes the biblical principal of "family." It promotes techniques like "time out" or "just talk to your toddler" and despises biblical principles of discipline. It pretends to be supportive of the family unit, but behind the scenes are forces working to divide and conquer. It shakes your hand and smiles in your face while slowly piercing your back with a dagger, and you never know what's hit you. Slowly you turn to walk away, thinking everything is going to be okay, when out of your daydream, you feel something warm and gooey oozing down your back or your chest. It's sticky to the touch, metallic to the taste, and just before you pass out or feel like you're about to faint, just before your heart ruptures, you realize you've been stabbed.

It speaks of unity and peace like the Antichrist in Revelations yet within the family unit; it causes war, disruption, and disharmony. It drags you in and out of courts more than church attendance by the host pastor during a weekly revival. It speaks of policies and procedures when it's to their advantage yet, it can never manage to manifest said policies and procedures to you. It can provide you with their representatives who are able to quote more law than the bible has scriptures, yet unlike the bible, they can never back up their case numbers, file numbers, and proceedings. It is just like its father, the Satan; it has many fooled into thinking it's a good thing, it's healthy, it's beneficial, and it's needed. It prides itself at doing what is in "the best interest of the child." However, it speaks only of the physical body and totally forgets the emotional and spiritual well-being of the child, but this is just what the Devil wants. Let's forget the spiritual child, forget the emotional child; if we take them away from their parents, we can rule them, break their spirits, and brainwash them then they will say just what we want them to say. Who needs parents when we have foster care? We promote unity, it says, but let's separate the parent from the child; let's not let them see each other for at least seventy-two hours or longer—maybe thirty days—that should be enough legal time to break the kid and torture the parent, to divide and conquer!

This is the year 2006, and surely this can't happen in the great United States of America! What is the meaning of all this blasphemy of a system so vast and so powerful? However, the system is corrupt and full of hidden truths, subtle lies, deceptive plots, and sullen schemes, and one would never know about them until one has been in the system. Whether by accident or factual information, once you've been thrown into the system, you're in for a life-changing experience that will never be forgotten, and hopefully, with the help of the almighty God, you'll come out of the system with minimal scars.

This system, called DFCS, stands for Demonic Forces Against Children's Spirits (DFACS). It may be called by a slightly different name in different states, but still the same department. It is full of social workers, caseworkers, supervisors, deputies, chief deputies, administrators, and directors, all attempting to fulfill a common goal "for the sake of the children," yet no one knows what the other is doing. Overwhelmed in paperwork, cases, policies, procedures, laws and bylaws, the right hand rarely knows what the left hand is doing. Under the dictation and protection of the law, DFCS sets out to judge, program you and your child, and tell you how to raise your child. Ironically, the assigned caseworkers and social workers usually don't have any children of their own, yet they are being paid to instruct you in child-rearing; they even have a backup plan to ensure you comply. These workers often lack the experience of having children of their own, yet they are paid to judge you and decide if you are fit to be a parent, something they know nothing about—*parenting*.

According to CPS (what I call Child Programming Services, not Child Protective Services), once you are charged with child abuse, you are guilty first and foremost, even if the court doesn't question the allegations. There is no such thing as an innocent parent when a child is suspect in a case of abuse. It doesn't matter if you have adopted a child with a tragic but realistic history of self-abusive behavior or if the child is your biological offspring. Even with documentation of your child's past and present, CPS workers are driven to prove you guilty, and the goal has nothing to do with "uniting the family unit." Strangely, many times, regardless of incompetence, ignorance, or innocence, DFCS and CPS have returned children back to true child abusers, while parents who are truly working hard at being «good parents" have had their children ripped from them and placed in foster care, pending investigations.

In November 2006, there was a case where a mother was charged with killing her two-year-old child. DFCS was aware of reports of abuse in the past, yet they allowed this child to remain with her biological mother. Sadly, it ended tragically in the death of the child. Was this incompetence, ignorance, or innocence? You be the judge. Despite reports and complaints from neighbors and visible marks noted by CPS, this child was still allowed to return to her parent. I wish I knew the mother's secret to proving to CPS and DFCS that she was worthy.

Have you ever had your heart, still pumping blood, ripped from your body while you walk around? Have you ever breathed yet felt no oxygen enter your lungs or seen the most beautiful sunset and felt nothing? Have you ever been surrounded by people in a church or football stadium yet felt totally alone in the world? Have you ever awakened in the morning to find a lump in your throat and a pit in your stomach, regretting another day? Or have you ever awakened dehydrated from crying yourself to sleep with drenched pillows cold and sticky against your skin? All this yet no one to speak to, no one is around, and you feel that even God has gone on vacation. How lonely or alone have you felt? Have you ever felt like dying? Was there ever a time in your life when all hell had broken loose around you, and knowing in your heart how much you love the Lord, you found yourself smack dab in the middle of the pit of hell? Have you ever wondered where is God, and how could He allow something like this to happen? Yet, God is in control, and through all the hell, he brings you out without the scent of fire or smoke. Have you ever felt loneliness so thick you can touch it because of the emptiness in your home?

The most priceless to a parent is his/her child. This holds especially true for the single parent with only one child. Whether taken by DFCS, CPS, or taken by death, to lose a child is most tragic in all of life. This is the foundation and reason for my story. May it impact you the way it impacted me. May it bless you, educate you, and shake up your emotions. I pray that while reading this book, you'll laugh, cry, get angry, get spiritual, get emotional, and let it refresh you and renew in you an awareness of a system that can strike the innocent just as quickly as the guilty. May you enter my story and my life and feel what I felt, hate what I hated and love what I loved. This is my story; may it penetrate the very depth of your soul and spirit and in the end, make you truly appreciate your gifts from God called *children*.

Let me take you on a journey through the system we so depend on for our children's welfare, called the Department of Family and Children Services (DFCS) or what I call Demonic Forces Against Children's Spirits. Allow me to take you where no man has gone before—exposed. As you read this book, cry if you must, laugh if you feel, and get angry if you can, but do continue to read this to the very end. Knowledge is power, and the power is yours to do with as you please. The information in this story is true, although the names have been changed to protect both the innocent and the not so innocent because for me to truly expose their identities would make me no better than they are. Are you ready to cry with me, feel my pain, and rejoice in my victory? Will you join me in making a difference after reading this book, or will you just close the book and comment on how good or bad it was? The bottom line is knowledge is still power, and you have it in your hands right now, so read on and be even more educated.

I appreciate you taking the time to read this book and share my experiences. I only ask that you share this information, especially with those who are considering adoption versus foster care. Read on, friend, and to God be the glory.

BOOK I.

THE BABY YEARS

CHAPTER 1. THE ABDUCTION

"Casting all your care upon him; for he careth for you."
1 Peter 5:7 KJV

According to Encarta Dictionary, "abduction" means "to snatch somebody away, to take somebody away by force or deception." Abduction also means "kidnap, seizure." This is what DFACS did with my baby, and sadly, it's legal!

The day was cold but sunny on April 10, 2006. Ironically, I remember it was the birthday of an old boyfriend who had died years ago. I was on my way to the car dealership to pick up my car from its routine service and then I was going to pick up my five-year-old son from school. I was standing in front of my service guy when I received the call on my cell phone from the school principal. Her words were short and to the point: "Isaiah's been taken by DFCS." I was stunned and numb, shocked, and could not believe my ears until she repeated it to me. I asked her when, and she advised me that they came to the school and took him around 2:30 p.m. It was now 5:15 p.m., so I asked why I was just getting the call. The principal gave the lame excuse that she did not have my pager number or cell number. Liar! I can't count the numerous times in a week the school had called me with complaints of my child's behavior. She then provided me with the name and number of the supervisor for CPS, whom I'll call Mr. Mudd. The principal made it sound as if it was no fault of the school that DFCS came to get my son; in fact, she acted as if she was as surprised as I was (what a performance).

I was paralyzed as I stood there in the office of my car service guy with mouth open and a now dead cell phone in hand; I needed the time for the blood to catch up with my brain and oxygenate it. My thoughts were about where my son was, what he must be thinking, what he must be going through, how abandoned he must be feeling now, not knowing where I was or why he was not coming home. I hated the school for its treachery and deception. I hated the way the principal handled both my son and me. I hated the way the system used a schoolteacher (who knew of sessions with my son and I to discuss his behavior) to call DFCS... what a *traitor!* I had a thousand thoughts going through my mind, and out of nowhere I remembered I needed to call the CPS number provided by the principal. I was surprised I still had the number as I did not remember writing it down. I advised my service guy at the dealership that I had to step outside to make a call. He asked if everything was okay as he'd known me for over two years; what could I say? Yes, no—all I could do was wave a hand and step outside.

I immediately called CPS, and my first question to Mr. Mudd was, "Where is my son?" He of course answered with a question. "What happened to your son? What did you do to him?" When I asked for clarification, he accused me of abusing my son and told me if he had his way, I would be in jail. I stood there in shock with my mouth opened as the blood drained from my face. I asked again, "Where is my son?" and he replied, "Somewhere safe!" Can you imagine somewhere safe being away from his mother? I was made to feel like a monster. I was never told where my son was, what he was going through, or what the circumstances were which required intervention by CPS in the first place. I was only given a time to meet with Mr. Mudd, the CPS caseworker, and a mediator, which of course came from DFCS. Mr. Mudd's words continued to ring in my ears and haunt my spirit long after our conversation was over. All I could hear was "He's somewhere safe," and I "ought to be in jail." I had a wicked headache, and my heart literally hurt. I was hungry, but I could not eat. I was tired, but I could not sleep, and my mind was miles away searching for my son.

I came home to an empty house, except for my pet cat. I'm used to having my son let the cat out of the room, but that day, it was my chore. I thought, *How long will they keep him? What is he doing now? How is he being treated?* Oh, how my heart hurt. My throat was dry, and my headache had grown, despite my Tylenol. How could this happen? Where could I find help? Who could I speak with and not feel like they would judge me inappropriately? I cried until there were no more tears left. I prayed until I ran out of words to say to God, who already knew the deal. I called two friends (my brother and sister in Christ) whom I considered to be family to me. They were as shocked as me, but at least they offered comforting words during the tragedy. There weren't many people I could speak with about it. I felt that even though I was a member and minister in one of the largest churches in Atlanta, God forbid I should call them. After over nineteen years at this church, I knew better than to spill my guts. They would never understand, and I would be treated like a leper. I prayed throughout the rest of the evening and each day prior to the pending meeting, which was two days away. I felt like God was so far away from me, yet I knew better than to think He was unaware or did not care about my situation. My family was all out of state, and they were the last people I wanted to know about this abduction; after all, some of my siblings thought my adoption was a big mistake in the first place, especially since I was single. Family tends to view you as the child they grew up with and not as the adult you've become.

The two days prior to my meeting with DFCS were the longest two days of my life. My nights were long with tear-soaked pillows, and even our cat missed having my son around. He seemed to sense something was wrong, which he tried to correct with his rough tongue attempting to lick some comfort into me. I struggled at work to put on a phony smile and positive attitude, and to this day, all I can say is that it was the Lord's doing, and it is marvelous in our sight. My heart ached for my son, and my thoughts were always on him, praying that the Lord would strengthen him and give him wisdom in dealing with his separation from me. This was something I could not speak about with everyone, and even my closest friend may or may not understand I was being accused of child abuse. This is something that is not tolerated, and even jail is a living hell for the person being persecuted for child abuse.

I'm not sure which was worst, being accused of child abuse or knowing that all the drama and sacrifices made to become an adopted parent was on the verge of being all for naught. After all, I took a sixteen-week course called MAPP training (Model Approach to Partnerships in Parenting), which was held every Tuesday evening for three hours. Each night, homework was given with the expectation of completing it before the next class. Although most of the homework was a no brainer, all the work required hours of quality time to complete, and it required taking a good look at your inner self. It was sometimes painful as I judged my ability to become a parent, especially a single parent. I would pray and hope that I was being obedient to God. On a consistent basis I looked for signs, clues, and signals indicating, or rather confirming, I was on the right track. I did not feel secure scheduling a counseling session with one of the ministers at my church, and I knew having a meeting with my pastor was impossible, so I called upon an old friend, mentor, and pastor who spoke with me in his office for almost two hours. I wanted scriptural backing for me adopting a child and being single doing it.

He reminded me that our Lord Jesus was adopted by Joseph, and Moses was adopted by Pharaoh's sister who was single, and the list goes on. My Tuesdays were full for sixteen weeks, rushing from work at 6:00 p.m. to be in class by 7:00 p.m., many times without eating. I'd questioned close friends and family about my decision to adopt and listened to their input concerning the matter. I read books on adoption versus foster parenting and spoke with couples who had done one or the other. I was the best student in the training class, finishing with a certificate, ribbon, and awards for good work; however, the MAPP training never prepared me for the actual adoption of my son.

One of the required homework assignments was that I had to create a family tree. I took precious time to create a family tree that would include my adopted child. I had to provide a biography of myself along with a picture which included information about my own family and siblings. I was expected to provide drawings of a family circle and what it meant, and I had to draw a social circle and tell what it meant. I was expected to bare my soul, sort of speak to assure the system that I was worthy of receiving a child. However, I was ready and willing to jump through hoops, walk the tightrope, or whatever it took to prove my ability to be a worthy parent. I knew without a doubt, my home would provide the love that no foster home or foster parent could provide. Despite all this and more, CPS thought I went through all this hell only to bring a child home and beat his brains out!

The abduction of my son was as sudden and unexpected as a thief in the night. I remember thinking about what clothes he was wearing and if I had put clean underwear on him, what coat did he have with him. I was concerned about his medicine since he was diagnosed with asthma five months prior to this abduction. Of course, DFCS and CPS didn't care about this, nor did they ask. I thought about how he was taken from the school—was it in front of a lot of people, did he cry, was there a big scene, were his classmates or other children present, and did anyone care? Oh, what my son must have been thinking; after all, I had promised my son that I would *never* leave him. I'm told one should not ever say never; however, at the time, I wasn't thinking about or considering the possibility of DFCS or CPS ripping him from me. My newly adopted son suffered from separation anxiety—the fear of being abandon by a parent or loved one—which is normal for children in the system called DFCS. Having been placed in the system as an infant, I had adopted him when he had just turned two years of age, ending his cycle of multiple foster homes.

On April 12, 2006, the meeting which would start the fire blazing was held in a small, uneventful dark room. This was called the TDM (Team Decision Making) meeting. The décor was very minimal and the atmosphere cold. After all, I really didn't expect red carpet treatment, but neither did I expect to feel like I was going to the guillotine. I was told to sit at one end of the small conference table, which I did with my brother in Christ, the only one I could trust who would not judge me and who knew me better than most. At the other end of the table sat Mr. Mudd, supervisor for CPS. To my right was the CPS caseworker whom I'll call Ms. Recore. To my left was the mediator whom I'll call Ms. Referee. There were no kind words spoken to open the meeting, and Mr. Mudd was straight to the point. "We took pictures, and if I had my way, I'd see to it that you were thrown in jail right now." My comment was, "Well, I'm glad you're not having your way, and I hope you're not planning to grill me here. Not having my son with me for the past couple of days is quite enough punishment." He went on and on about how terrible child abuse is, asking what did I do and what was I thinking. I just looked at him. Ms. Recore had the nerve to say with her winey voice, "It looks like you bit him," and then *she grinned a little!* I barked at her, "I assure you I'm not a cannibal!" My brother nudged me under the table to keep cool. Mr. Mudd then asked me if I wanted to see the pictures; of *course* I wanted to see the pictures! What a dumb question! When I saw the pictures, I wanted to die. My brother and I both looked at each other in shock. There was my son in one picture, shirt off flexing both arms to show muscles and grinning from ear to ear. The next picture he was smiling showing a bruise on his wrist the size of a half dollar. I asked Ms. Recore if this was the bruise she thought looked like a bite mark, and she said yes. Clearly, it looked just like a bruise sustained when someone hits his wrist on a hard object, which is exactly what my son had done during one of his many fits called temper tantrums. I asked where the teeth marks were if the bruise looked like a bite, but of course she had no answer.

The mediator finally spoke up, stating she knew how hard it was for a single parent to raise a child in this day and age, and sometimes it's easy to let our tempers get the best of us. She suggested perhaps I needed to get help with anger management. She further stated that she knew it could be very challenging when you don't have an outlet (as if she knew my way of life). I asked her if she was a parent, and she said no! Yet, she assumed she knew how I was feeling, how I lived my life, and what I needed. The meeting had me wanting to get an Uzi and blow both DFCS and CPS away; then maybe I'd go to anger management. How dare they sit and judge me and my character, and two of the three people representing the system didn't even have children of their own!

I thought this was as good a time as any to start from the beginning and tell them a little about my son's history. I was angry at even having to do this because if Fulton County had done its job and communicated with Clayton County, then they would already be aware of my son's history. You see, when my adoption proceedings were initiated with the MAPP training, I lived in Clayton County; however, by the time I was notified about the placement of my son, over a year had lapsed, and I had purchased a home in Fulton County. The supervisor for adoptions at Clayton provided me with a number to call Fulton County DFCS to schedule a home review or assessment. This is when a social or caseworker comes to your home and sees if it is fit for a child, but Fulton DFCS never did this. In fact, when I called the number provided to me, I was told, "Well, I don't know why Clayton told you to call us. We have enough problems of our own. Since they started your adoption, they should finish it." Can you imagine being told something like this? I immediately called the supervisor at Clayton County and told her what I was told. Of course, she apologized and said that they would handle it. Now, years later, Fulton DFCS who knew nothing about my son's history of self-abusive behaviors and catabolic fits of rage, sat accusing me of such a heinous act—child abuse and neglect. Unfortunately, all his records were sealed, and there was no way of pulling up the history. When Fulton had access to this information, they refused to do a simple house visit and complete the adoption. However, I had kept every single piece of documentation from all the numerous daycares, pre-school, after-school care programs, and summer programs that my son had attended and was kicked out of due to his behavior. I had well over forty-two pages documenting exactly what his behavior displayed and why they could no longer keep him at their facilities. The documentation came from the schoolteachers, principals, directors, and administrators. I remembered all the numerous times I was heartbroken when my son and I were repeatedly rejected by all the schools and educational facilities. I sat accused of something I would never do and had evidence to justify my innocence. I presented my documents to everyone present; I had made sure I had copies to go around. Mr. Mudd told me they would review all the information I presented. I thought what a relief that was—at least they were going to review the information, and maybe they would provide me with help.

I begged Mr. Mudd not to place my son back in foster care as that would undo all the years I had spent trying to get the system way of living out of my son. He asked if I had a family member who would care for him, and my brother spoke up. Mr. Mudd then asked for all his credentials, as well as his wife's, such as address, social security numbers, etc. I explained to him that my brother was present throughout all the proceedings prior to and the day of the adoption and that he was an uncle to my son. All the information was in vain, however, because at the end of the meeting, Mr. Mudd frankly stated that he had changed his mind, and my son would be put back in foster care for thirty days. He looked at me as if to say, "Now there!" as if he really wanted to stick it to me, and he did! I asked if he thought it was in the best interest of my son to stay with strangers instead of family. His remark was that it was the least he could do for Isaiah, as if he was doing my son a favor. I was told of the upcoming court date, and if I wanted my son back, I would need to comply. The meeting ended as abruptly as it began. I think I tasted bile in my mouth and felt like I'd just came from Satan's lair.

I left the meeting broken, feeling like I'd just gone nine rounds with Ali and most importantly, without my son. My brother tried to encourage me, but what words can be spoken when a parent loses a child? It doesn't matter how that loss is achieved. I went home, but it no longer felt like home. I took a shower for over an hour, but I still felt dirty from all the filth and derogatory remarks at the meeting. I lay down on my bed, but I wasn't sleepy. I was angry, restless, confused, and exhausted, all at the same time. I kept telling myself that God is in control and there is a reason for all this, but then what in hell was the reason? I was numb, and I think I still must have been in a state of shock because I really was not in tune with my senses. I could not feel. I was not hungry. I couldn't blame anyone for this happening, not even myself—it just happened! All the whats, whys, and whens were lost in the wind. There were no questions, there were no answers, and there were no reasons—*it just happened!* One thing I do know is that it was sent from the pit of hell and was meant to take me out! However, every Christian knows that the Devil is a liar, and though I might fall, I shall arise! It would take time for me to arise from this pit of despair, confusion, and loneliness. Oh, how I wished I had someone that I could just vent to about the incident. It's times like those that I truly missed being married. Sitting up alone in my bedroom looking at the cat somehow did not give me any peace or relaxation. All I could think about was that these people were really out to get me, and what was I supposed to do and where should I start? I was embarrassed and ashamed that such an incident could even take place in my life, and it was something I would have to live with for the rest of my life. I never would have imagined myself being investigated by the same institution I once thought was the greatest for children. I was, at one time, in full support of them. However, this was when I was going through the process to become an adoptive parent. Little did I know about the behind-the-scenes drama, the deception and misconception, the turnover in staff and botched meetings, or meetings that were supposed to be but never happened, and no one knew why. The system set up in each state to protect children is the same system that rips children from their families and loved ones, often unannounced, all in the name of safety. Ironically, although we all know that there are children who are truly being abused, it seems that these are the very children that this system lets slip through the cracks. How many times have we heard about a caseworker being aware of a child being abused yet has allowed that child to return home when the evidence was as clear as the child not wanting to be with the parent, screaming and crying at seeing the parent, or a neighbor and sometimes even a family member reported the abuse with obvious signs and symptoms?

What was I to do now? I mean, I'd seen child abuse in my profession. I'm mandated by law to report it as a healthcare professional.

I've read about it, heard it on the news, even treated abused toddlers, but never did I think I would ever be accused of abuse. I know for a fact that people, even Christians, aren't so forgiving, and it doesn't matter about being innocent, having a record expunged, or having the case thrown out of court; once you've been labeled, you're treated differently. For years I've worked with children and in the children's ministry at church; however, now they find other things for me to do. People in leadership are careful not to hurt your feelings or leave you suspicious of the change in assignment, but you always know, and to keep from being called an immature Christian, you keep the hurt buried inside. You don't discuss it with anyone except God, and you think, *Well, since God allowed it to happen, maybe working with children is no longer what He wants me to do.* Yet God did not make a mistake when He gave me my son. He didn't make a mistake when He chose me to become a parent. After all, by the time my son came into my life, I had long given up on the thought of becoming a parent, and I had long completed the training at DFCS, and I did not pray for a child. However, people don't think of these things when they've heard of your misfortune, and if you're an extrovert, "speak your mind" person like I am, they will more than likely think against you and not for you. If I was quiet and introverted, then the thought may have been, *No, she could never hurt a child.* Why, she wouldn't hurt a flea. I'm in the performing arts, dance, and drama, and during productions and recitals, with over fifty children involved, you may hear me yelling, "QUIET," but that doesn't mean I have the potential for being a child abuser. For weeks, I did not go to church because I did not want everyone who saw me to ask where my son was, and I did not want to have to lie to them. What was I to say—he's in a foster home?? I can think of at least ten people *at church* who envied my being blessed with a child, and even some family members had doubt; after all, I was single and very active. Unfortunately, the last help I wanted during my ordeal was from my church. Not to put my church down, but three years prior, it was impossible just getting an appointment to see my pastor for counseling to discuss my plan to adopt. Most importantly, I would know of other people's business, love affairs, adultery, and misuse of church funds, things I should not have known about and did not even ask about, yet I knew. I certainly did not want my business out in the church, especially when I knew they would not be supportive of me, so I stayed away and prayed and prayed and prayed. I asked God to help me forgive my church for being so unapproachable, and the sad thing is that it's not even the pastor making decisions, but those placed in leadership, making them for him. I do think things would have been different if I was able to speak with my pastor. In any event, I remember my pastor saying years ago, "Without struggle, there is no growth," and I thought, *Boy I must be getting ready for a lot of growing*, because I was in a major struggle which was to last for years. Being accused of child abuse by DFCS is just the tip of the iceberg; by the time they are finished with you, you're so broken, that if you're not strong and don't know the Lord, you'll be too broken to even care for your child if the decision is to return your child to you. There is no such thing as restoration of the parent with DFCS, but then again, sometimes I feel there is no such thing as restoration in my church either. Once you've been sat down from participating in a ministry for whatever the reason, then you are sat–period. So, there I was, broken, not able to go to church because of the potential of and fear of gossip, not able to see my child or even get a report of how he was really doing because of DFACS, and not able to get on with my life, if you want to call it life. I felt like my life was just ripped from me. However, with all this, there was a good side; there was still one friend who stuck closer than a brother–my Lord, Jesus.

CHAPTER 2. THE CONCEPTION

"For lo, thou shalt conceive, and bear a son."
Judges 13:5 KJV

The day was warm and sunny for October 7th when I conceived my son in 2002. I was busy at work when I received a 911 page from the Department of Family and Children Services. It was near the end of my day shift on a Friday when I got the call at the hospital. I was informed by the caseworker for adoption that they needed placement for a two-year-old boy, and felt I was the perfect fit. My heart was racing. They wanted me to come to the office immediately. My coworkers all knew that in the past I had gone through training and preparation for adoption. It had been well over a year, and I hadn't given it much thought. I was excited by the call and the possibility of becoming a new mother. Could it be that after all this time I was finally to become a mom? I quickly left work and as I took the long drive to the DFCS office, there were many thoughts running through my mind. I wondered what he would look like, if he would be healthy, and could I actually pull this motherhood thing off? What would my family say when the plan for years finally manifested? Was I really ready for this, Lord? Could I afford a child? Would he love me, and could I love him? What should I say to him? Would he be smart? Finally, I called my sister in Tennessee and said, "Let's pray." We prayed all the way to the office asking God for guidance and a confirmation that this child was indeed meant to be my son. I remember my was heart pounding, my mouth was dry, my respirations had increased, and while this wasn't marriage, it was motherhood.

I arrived at the DFCS office, and no sooner than walking through the door, I was met by both the caseworker and social worker for adoption. In the reception area playing with some toy was the cutest little boy I'd ever seen. They called him over to where we were standing, and he was not shy by any means. I bent down to him and asked his name which he promptly blurted out in his toddler language. I stretched out my arms and asked if I could have a hug which he was too happy to give. As I picked him up in my arms, he patted me on the back and said, "Momma." As my eyes welled with tears, I took it as a sign that this child was mine. I noticed the social worker and caseworker standing side by side with abated breath, encouraging the union. DFCS was aware that over a year prior, when I initially started adoption proceedings, I specifically requested a child whose parental rights had been terminated. This is what they call a TPR (Termination of Parental Rights). Funny, as a nurse, I'm use to TPR being temperature, pulse, and respirations. Anyway, I did not want to get my emotions tied up with a child only to have him or her snatched away from me by parents or family members who changed their minds years later. Both the caseworker and social worker assured me that parental rights had indeed been terminated. They practically begged me to take this child, stating that the shelter was full, and both spouses of each worker had forbidden them from coming home again with the child. That was all that was said, and they really did not have to beg me to take the child. I no sooner accepted this child who was to become my son, when they quickly thrust a dilapidated grey, flimsy suitcase into my hand. Inside were two Pampers, a short and shirt set, and a pair of shoe boots which were clearly too large for the child. They walked me to the car, and one of the workers ran back to get a car seat for me. At this time, it was almost 5:00 p.m., and I sensed they were anxious to leave. As I placed my son in the car seat, I saw both workers standing next to each other with clasped hands held up to their mouths, giggling and whispering to each other, "Ooh, he's not crying. This is a match." I asked for the paperwork regarding this child and was told, "They will have the paperwork ready for you on Monday." I was shocked and horrified at the same time. With bulging eyes, I asked, "Suppose I get stopped by the police or somebody. How would I justify having this child with me?" "Oh, don't worry," they told me. "You won't get stopped, and if you do, just have them call us." Clearly, I could see that they were dead serious as they did not have one piece of paper in their hands. Reluctantly, I got in my car and drove off with my son in the back seat, praying that this was legitimate, even though it felt like a legal kidnapping.

I drove to a nearby Kroger's to pick up some foods fit for a toddler. My son was very talkative, so I asked him what he liked to eat. Everything he named was pure junk food, chips, candy, gummy bears, cookies, etc. I pulled into a parking space next to an opening where they keep the shopping carts. I got out of the car and went around to lift my son out of the car seat. As I stood him up on the ground to pull one of the shopping carts free, he lifted both his arms for me to pick him up. I said, "Okay, baby. Wait until Mommy gets this cart. Before I could finish my sentence, my son threw himself down on the bare concrete and proceeded to produce a blood curdling scream while thrashing his arms and legs on the ground. I was horrified as I quickly picked him up to keep him from injuring himself. As I attempted to sit him in the cart, he proceeded to punch me in the chest and head. It was difficult sitting him in the cart because he arched his back, preventing his legs from going into the part of the cart for legs. All I could think of was the woman at the mall who, two weeks prior, had been carted off to jail by the police because she popped her daughter during a temper tantrum in the parking lot of the mall. Unfortunately, it was caught on the mall camera in the parking lot. Once I finally got him in the cart, he continued to scream and cry, hitting his arms on the handle of the shopping cart and saying, "Ouch!" but continued with this abusive behavior. I bribed him to shut him up, telling him I'd buy him cookies, and we were going into the store to get cookies. This seemed to quiet him, so I purchased the Goldfish crackers and tore them open to keep him quiet. He continued to want to scream and whine as we passed items he wanted. I intentionally stayed away from the junk food aisle. I was met with stares and curiosity as I proceeded to the cashier with my temperamental son. My trip to Kroger's to shop for my toddler was the shortest in the history of shopping.

By the time I got back to my car, unloaded, and strapped my son in the car seat, I felt like I went a round with Ali. I was exhausted, and I was angry. My eye was slightly swollen from his punches, and my chest was sore from his kicks. Clearly, those workers at DFCS knew the behavior of this child, and they kept this vital information from me. Now I understood why they were having their prayer vigil while I was strapping my son in the car at DFCS. I now understood why their spouses told them not to bring the child back home. The time was 5:45 p.m. on a Friday, and if I knew they were still at the office, I would have driven the child, suitcase, and car seat right back to DFCS. I looked at my new son in the rearview mirror who was now falling asleep after his temper tantrum or rather, his fit of rage. I wondered what happened in his young life to cause him to be so angry. I had planned to deal with whatever over the weekend, and first thing Monday I would be at the front door of DFCS for some vital information and an explanation.

My first stop was to my brother's place where my son met his aunt, uncle, cousins, and granny. I had my heart in my throat in anticipation when my son would fly off the handle again. Since I arrived in time for dinner, of course Mom immediately went to fix a plate for my son. On his plate was chicken and corn kernels. He picked up each kernel with his fingers, leaving his spoon on the plate. I went over to him to show him how to use the spoon to eat his corn. I placed the spoon in his hand, but before I could go any further, he threw the spoon across the table, barely missing Mom. When I rinsed the spoon and attempted to show him again, he threw himself out of the chair and started his temper tantrum. I moved him into the middle of the floor away from the dining room table to prevent him injuring himself. We all just kept our eye on him but allowed him to go through his tantrum. My visit to my brother's was the shortest in the history of my family.

First thing Monday, I was at the office of DFCS with my son. The first question asked by the staff was if I was bringing the child back. Everyone in the office knew my son and his fits of rage, but no one felt it important enough to share this information with the prospective parent for fear of rejection. Ironically, both the social worker and caseworker for adoptions had called out! I couldn't believe my ears. The worker filling in for them assumed that I knew the history of my son, and she started spilling her guts. She was a real talker, probably the office gossiper. She said, "Lawd, when I heard Isaiah had been placed, I said oh she'll be bringing him back. Um, see there. You back." She continued to go on and on without taking a breath about his behaviors. When she shut up long enough to see the horror on my face, she then realized that I had been clueless about his history, but of course, by then it was too late, and I had been unintentionally well-informed. To protect my son, I will not divulge his history much because, after all, this book is not about him per se, but rather about the Department of Family and Children Services. However, trust me when I say that the information provided to me after the fact was mind boggling and vital for me to know as a new parent. I felt that the DFCS case and social workers for adoption made a shady attempt to conceal information in order to quickly pass this child off so that neither one of them would be stuck with him over the weekend. They wanted him out of the office so fast that they didn't even take the time to complete the paperwork, and worst, they both called out the following business day. While I had demanded to speak with their supervisor, I found her to be clueless as to what was going on and what had gone on. She wasn't friendly toward me, and you would think that I was the enemy instead of the one who had taken a troubled child off their hands and out of the system. She appeared to be upset at being disturbed and called out of her office. She took her time coming into the foyer area where I was patiently waiting to speak with her. However, as stated earlier, she was clueless regarding my adoption. She asked that I give her time to pull the paperwork. My response was to ask what paperwork since I wasn't given anything. She assured me that even though they should have given me papers, they had to have documentation in the office, and she was going to pull those papers and determine exactly what was done or should have been done. I told her I had all the time in the world and would wait. After what seemed like hours later, she came back into the foyer with the papers I should have been given that Friday. In addition to this, she provided me with a letter giving me permission to take my son out of town since I had planned a vacation to Florida prior to being informed of my motherhood. My adoption wasn't finalized, so I needed permission to take my son out of state. Ms. Supervisor wasn't a bit apologetic at my not being informed of my son's past. In fact, she acted like it really wasn't a concern at all. *How ignorant*, I thought but then had to consider the source, and I am referring to a supervisor who was clueless about her staff's job productivity and activity.

I left the office with my son, having decided that to place him back into this system would be like the murder of an innocent child. Clearly the system was capable of major errors and not as "safe" as I had thought during my training. The drive back home was less eventful as I had thoughts of being at the beach and introducing my son to the sand and the sea. I was still a bit bewildered regarding the policies and procedures of the Department of Family and Children Services, but for now, my plan was to lay all this aside as I focused on bonding with my new son by the sea. After over a year, conception had taken place, and motherhood was becoming a reality, but honestly, I would not have been any better prepared if it had taken place earlier.

CHAPTER 3. THE THREE-RING CIRCUS

"No weapon that is formed against thee shall prosper; and every tongue that shall rise against thee in judgment thou shalt condemn."
Isaiah 54:17

April 14, 2006, was the day of my first appearance in court for my so-called "Probable Cause Hearing for alleged cruelty to children. First of all, I don't have children. I have a child, but it is all the same in the court of law. I couldn't sleep the night before, and when I finally fell asleep, I woke way too early. I used this time to pray for divine intervention, strength, and the return of my son. After all my praying, I still felt physically weak, possibly related to my lack of a balanced diet. Spiritually, I felt like I was on a roller coaster ride, but I knew this was a trick of the enemy, and God was on my side. I kept telling myself that God would not allow this child in my life only to have him removed from me. I had two days to find an attorney to represent me in court. The one recommended to me did not provide the security and assurance I wanted and needed, but at the time, I really did not have a choice. She was very clear about having her money upfront, and I feared if I did not deliver, she would provide shoddy work, if any. I took my mortgage and paid her the initial $1,000, along with over forty-two pages of documentation of my son's self-abusive behaviors as documented by various teachers in various schools for the past four years.

Thank God for the brother he placed in my life who was there for me or else I don't know if I would have had the strength to stand. My throat was dry, and my heart was stuck somewhere between my sternum and larynx. I was at the court early, and as I sat in the hallway, I wondered if I would see my son, how he would respond to me, how he would look, what the judge would say... just all kinds of thoughts. I noticed how clean the hallway was, the wood panel walls blending in with the floors. I looked out the many windows at the city I grew to love and wondered what had gone wrong. It was a sunny day, and the sun was literally beaming through those windows, making the hallway hot. I watched as attorneys paraded up and down the halls, going into one courtroom and coming out, just to go into another courtroom. I saw families leaving the courtroom in tears. I sat among other families with children who had fear in their eyes. I saw the families who had sat with me for what seemed like hours go into a courtroom and come out in tears, and I wondered if they lost their children? Had the court taken their children? There wasn't a family present who did not leave in tears. I was a nervous wreck inside, but on the outside, I knew I had to maintain my cool. With all this drama going on around me, my attorney was nowhere in sight which caused me yet another concern. Where was she? Thank God the court was running late as it was already over an hour past the designated time, and I had to be present.

From the right corner of my eye, I heard footsteps running, and an adult attempted to stop my child from running down the hall; however, he broke free and did a 100-yard dash toward me. It was my son. "Mommy!" I heard him yell, and he did not care where he was or who was with him. He ran in to my arms, beaming and squeezing my neck so tight. The next thing he said was, "Look what DFCS brought me." He was wearing a SpongeBob short set. He looked pale to me. I asked how he was doing, but I no sooner started to speak with him when several people rushed over to me and quickly whisked him away from me. I sat in horror as the child advocate pulled him aside and spoke to him in the hall. My brother and I eyed each other because clearly this was a mistake, and my son was not supposed to even see me. However, the child advocate no sooner finished speaking with him when two other people started questioning him. Minutes later, a tall and slender, long-haired blond woman strode down the hall toward my son. She walked with an air of authority, and clearly, she was the one in charge, evidenced by the way everyone else was responding to her. I later learned that she was the SAAG (Special Assistant Attorney General). She also pulled my son aside and spoke to him, and I saw he was becoming loud and restless with her, so she had a toy truck which she used to bribe him to be quiet as she marched him down the hall and out the door into a private room. My brother and I took all this in silently. Approximately fifteen minutes later, my son came running back to me through the door, and I heard the SAAG say to the child advocate, who was attempting to stop him from running to me, to "just let him go."

My son was sitting on my lap, hugging my neck and excited about a police officer who had told him that milk would make him strong. My son told my brother and me that the officer also asked him about his bruise. While we were speaking, this officer came over to me smiling and asked if I was Ms. Wilson (the teacher at my son's school who reported me to DFCS), but before I could answer, my son blurted out excitedly, "This is my mommy!" I saw the blood drain from the officer's face, and he went pale as he lost his smile. He asked me to go with him for questioning, and when I referred him to my lawyer, his response was "Oh, you have an attorney?" I could tell he was really surprised. Thank God that just at that moment, my attorney finally did show up and after introductions, the SAAG, officer, child advocate, and my attorney were in a conversation at the other end of the hall. My son was again whisked away to speak with the judge in chambers. When they had finished questioning him, he once again managed to slip away from them and came through the court doors to me. He told his uncle and me that he had spoken with the judge who asked him what had happened. So, I asked my son if he told them the truth about his "falling out" and hitting himself. He answered, "No, Mommy!" with his eyes wide open. When I asked him why, he responded, "Mommy, I don't want to go to jail!" I then asked him, "Who told you that?" and my son replied that the officer who told him about the milk told him not to tell anybody that he falls out because he could go to jail. I don't know who was more shocked—my brother or I. Ironically, the officer stepped out of the court shortly after, and my son pointed him out to us.

Finally, it was my turn to enter the court and face the judge. He was a thin elderly Caucasian man with a sense of humor when it concerned the SAAG, whom he apparently liked and knew very well. They both had an exchange of cordial greetings and chuckles, and I knew then I had lost the possibility of coming home with my son. In addition, I sat there watching this woman to whom I had paid my mortgage say little to nothing in my defense. The SAAG walked circles around her, and I was even more shocked at her poor line of questioning; in fact, one of the questions that she presented to the CPS caseworker, Ms. Recore, worked against me, not for me. I thought, how stupid of her to even bring up such a question. The forty-two-page documentation was *never presented in court*; and my attorney didn't even bring it up. When I later asked her why, she said this was not the court for the evidence. Clearly, everything the SAAG requested, she got. The whole proceeding was over before it had begun, with the judge stating he believed my son would be safe in foster care for now, pounding the gavel and dismissing us. The years I'd worked with my son attempting to get DFCS out of his system was flushed down the toilet in a matter of hours. As we exited the court, my son was, of course, right outside the door waiting for me. When I told him I could not bring him home, he burst out in tears. The SAAG seeing this accused me of upsetting my son and being insensitive. What did she expect? Was I to lie to my son? I heard her say to her colleagues that she was going to see that my son stayed in foster care, to which I responded that if he remained in foster care, then they (DFCS) could keep him as I was not willing to start all over breaking through all his many barriers and obstacles placed on him by the system called DFACS. She was shocked at my remark, and I knew she would later take it out of context to use against me but at that time, I did not care. I took pleasure in seeing the shock on her face as it turned red because she did not expect me to have over-heard her. Sadly, at the end of the day, like the many families I had witnessed earlier that morning, I too left the court in tears, and my son went back to the foster home.

April 25, 2006, was my second court hearing. This was to decide my final fate and if my son would ever be returned to me. As with the first court appearance, this too was like a three-ring circus. As my brother and I entered the hall of the court, we witnessed the CPS caseworker, Ms. Recore, sitting on a bench with her colleagues show-ing my son's naked pictures! I was shocked to say the least. We over-heard her say, "She ain't gittin' him back. She's gon' to jail." All I could do was look at her and pray—for vengeance! There she sat with her two coworkers on either side, eyeballing me and rolling their eyes at me, a giggle here and a whisper there. Ms. Recore sat with her one tooth showing in the smirk on her face, weave out of place, run over penny loafers supporting a weight of over 200 pounds, and a long dress that looked like an army tent, taking pleasure at my sadness. She must have been a miserable person herself to take pleasure in a child being separated from his parent. They were all just chatter-boxes, loud and unprofessional, and none of them seemed to care that we heard every word, nor did they care that my son's pictures were being displayed in a very public place where other families were present. If my brother and I could see and hear, I'm sure those sitting next to us also could. I was so humiliated, angry, violated, and helpless, but my brother kept reminding me to do whatever it takes to get me son back, so if this meant keeping my mouth shut and being humiliated, so be it.

In the deprivation petition filed April 18th but presented in court, the SAAG documented that my son was in need of protection and was deprived due to the following conditions: he "is without parental care, control and supervision," "he was being physically abused by his mother," that upon entering the ruling at the Probable Cause Hearing the mother responded by stating that, "you can just keep him then" (I knew she would take my words out of content), "the mother upset the child by telling him he would not be coming home for a long time," legal custody should be granted to Fulton County Department of Family and Children Services (the same department that refused to service me when I was initially placed with my son), and finally she lied and stated that "reasonable and significant efforts have been made by the department and/or other appropriate agencies to preserve and/ or reunify the family prior to placement of the child in foster care." What a blatant lie! Needless to say, I was totally outraged by the deprivation petition. Absolutely nothing was done to prevent my son from going in to foster care. Even though my brother was present and provided them with all the information they needed to allow my son to go home with family, we were denied. It didn't matter that his auntie (my brother's wife) was also an attorney and would never do anything to compromise the system or her job or her license. However, the SAAG not only got away with this documentation, but she was backed by the law. I was outraged, but my sorry attorney told me that there was nothing I could do about it, and it really meant nothing. It was just a bunch of words to make the case strong. At that point, I was determined to do something about it, with or without my attorney's help.

Ironically, the child advocate did get the opportunity to review the documents I had submitted, and I overheard her comment, "Oh, my God. This is a bad child!" Now I disagree that he was a bad child; he just had major behavioral challenges which was due to being born in an unstable environment and thrown into a dysfunctional system which lacked support, stability, and security for a newborn. However, even this was a breakthrough, considering that the advocate was not for me but for my son, yet she was empathetic to what I was and had been going through. In addition, I had a female judge who did not appear to be so buddy-buddy with the SAAG. My attorney (I was surprised she even showed up since she had not contacted or consulted with me since the last court appearance) advised me not to worry about the wording in the deprivation petition; however, I was finding it hard to believe anything she had to say to me. I even had to call her and remind her of the court date and time. I could not believe that she was absolutely clueless concerning my court date.

When it was time for me to appear before the judge, my brother and I filed into the courtroom along with the attorneys and CPS caseworker, Ms. Recore. The SAAG was so effective with depicting me as a monster I would have gladly given her an Oscar, except for the fact that most of what she had to say were blatant lies. My attorney once again had little to say in my defense, but I thank God for providing me with a judge who had wisdom. I think she saw that my attorney was a novice when it came to dealing with juvenile court proceedings. The last words of the SAAG were that my son should never be returned to me and was safer with DFCS, and she reiterated my words spoken in the previous court, that they (meaning DFCS) could "just keep him." Thankfully, the judge asked me if I had anything to say; of course I did. I proceeded to start from the very day of my adoption when I was given this bundle of joy without any of the critical historical informa-tion needed to care for my son, nor was I provided any documents. The judge then asked if I had received an adoption packet. I told her that I didn't even know that such a packet existed. I further told her of Fulton County's DFCS refusal to service me once placement was established because, since the initiation of my adoption which took place in Clayton County, I had purchased a home in Fulton County; therefore, Fulton DFCS refused to finalize my adoption. The current help and resources I had in place were solely due to my own home-work and networking to get help I knew was needed for both my son and me. The judge was impressed with all I had to say and what I had already initiated toward getting much needed help for my son. She strongly encouraged the CPS caseworker to expedite the investiga-tion to assure I get the resources needed, so my son could quickly be returned to me. I asked the judge if she could also make Fulton DFCS contact Clayton DFCS to obtain the facts as it related to my son's history to expedite closure. I had requested Clayton to contact Fulton to discuss my son's past since his records had been sealed. Clayton DFCS had made several calls and left messages but none of the calls were returned by Fulton DFCS or CPS… can you imagine? What a mess—the two systems could not even come together for the sake of a child, my son. The judge granted my request and of course I requested to see my son, which she also granted. Lastly, I told the judge of my concern regarding all the verbiage in the deprivation petition written by the SAAG. I told her that most of the information documented in the petition was not the truth, and I had evidence. The judge advised me that if I obtained a copy of the petition and a copy of the court transcript and submitted it along with my concerns, she would consider reviewing it. She also warned me that I would need to pay her staff for the copy of the transcript, and I assured her that this would not be a problem. I could almost feel my attorney glaring at me from behind, but this was my life we were discussing, and at that point, I cared little about what she thought or what she had to say for that matter. She was a waste of my hard-earned money.

My second visit to see my son was to occur on April 27, 2006, at the DFCS office in Fulton County. I waited *three hours* at the office for my son. There was another miscommunication, and instead of my son meeting me for our visit, he was at forensic for further questioning, which was scheduled at the same time of our visit. No one with DFCS knew what the other was doing. The caseworker had gone to the school to pick up my son, and when she could not find him at the school, there was confusion as to which forensic center he was taken to. When I finally got to see my son, he was wearing pants three times his size, possibly pants belonging to one of the foster children he was staying with. He had a large goose egg in the center of his forehead, and both of his knees were slightly bloody and skinned, but no one had bothered to clean his wounds. He stated that he had fallen at the foster home. My son also told me that he had thrown up the night before. I asked what he had for dinner, and he told me hot wings and French fries, something he didn't eat at our home. I cooked wholesome meals, and fast foods were a luxury. He had a runny nose and felt feverish; he had had two nosebleeds at the foster home related to stress and complained of feeling nauseous and coughing at night. I asked the caseworker to allow me to run home to get his prescription medication for his asthma, since I did not live far from the office. DFACS never bothered to investigate any health issues prior to placement in a foster home. They never asked me about his health or if he was on any medications; they just did not care. The caseworker allowed me to get his medication to give to the foster parents. She also told me that the foster parents requested her to ask me to speak to my son regarding his behavior at the school. The foster parents were complaining that the school was calling them practically every day regarding his behavior, something I'd had to deal with for four and a half years. To this I laughed and told her that I would not speak to my son regarding his behavior. It was his behavior that currently had *me* under investigation, yet DFCS and CPS chose to believe that my son was being abused. I choose to spend my short time with him loving him and assuring him that we would be back together soon. I saw my son with multiple issues in foster care, yet the SAAG and the court felt he was safer in a foster home instead of with his family. Our second visit was bittersweet, leaving me starting all over again, missing him more and going home to an empty house and tear-soaked pillows at night.

I was so angry with the teacher, Ms. Wilson, at my son's school who overreacted because she saw a bruise on his wrist. I was especially angry with both DFCS and CPS for overreacting and placing my son in foster care, instead of allowing him to stay with family. How silly of me to think that they would do the right thing on behalf of my son. What a corrupt system for our children. Statistics show that in various states, when CPS was audited and investigated, that they were found doing unfair fiscal practices, such as taking non-abused children so they could benefit from the federal dollars, or "double dip" by taking money from the state or feds for the same things they were charging the parents for through child support dollars. No wonder they come in like a bunch of barracudas at the ring of a call alleging child abuse. The deceitful financial practices of CPS should be stopped as they are draining the federal Social Security Fund by taking money for services parents are forced into with threats of not seeing their children again if they don't comply. Parents are forced to take classes like anger management, therapy classes, and counseling referrals to be done during working hours which means missed time from work and decreased pay. This is a demand placed on parents while being separated from their children, a demand that could take months or even years to complete during a separation from our children. We are victimized by this system that makes a profit by holding our children longer and receives "bonuses" when they don't return them to us. Caseworkers and social workers are often guilty of fraud. They withhold evidence as Ms. Recore did with my documents and fabricate evidence as they seek to terminate parental rights.

A certain senator representing a district in Georgia investigated the practices of DFCS and CPS and found some startling statistics. This senator evidenced corrupt practices in both departments. Further, The Adoption and the Safe Families Act, which were started by President Bill Clinton, offered cash "bonuses" for every child adopted out of foster care. In order to receive these, what the senator calls "adoption incentive bonuses," more children are needed by the local CPS. The children are the "merchandise" which must be in abundance, so the buyers will have plenty to choose from. Some counties give a $4,000 bonus for each child adopted, and if the child is special needs, an additional $2,000 is provided. The employees work to keep federal dollars flowing and therefore "double dip," which continues as long as the child is out of the home. When the child is placed from foster care to a new family, "adoption bonus funds" are available. When a child has to be placed in a mental health facility on drugs each day, more funds are involved. *There are no financial resources or promotion to reunite the family.*

According to the senator, separating families has become a growing business because the local governments have become use to having taxpayer dollars to balance their expanding budgets. CPS and juvenile courts use a confidentiality clause to protect their decisions and keep the funds flowing. After all, look who's being paid—lawyers, court investigators, caseworkers, judges, foster parents, counselors, therapists, court personnel, psychologists, psychiatrists, forensic staff, and the list goes on. The social workers are the key or the "glue" that holds this corrupt system together and fund the children's attorneys, court, and many other jobs including the DFCS attorney or SAAG. All are using the children in state custody to provide job security. The senator stated uncertainty of the possibility of the system even being reformed, and it cannot be trusted. In the senator's investigation, it was learned that the system does not serve the people, but rather obliterates families and children simply because it has the power to do so. I thank God for a senator who can so clearly see the corruption that undergirds DFCS and CPS—a system that is broken beyond repair. DFCS has become a "protected empire built on taking children and separating families." At best, it is "legal kidnapping and ineffective policies," to quote the senator. Reportedly, the senator has worked approximately 300 cases statewide and is convinced that there is no accountability or responsibility in the system, and I totally agree, speaking from firsthand experience. No one told me of expectations surrounding a CPS investigation. I was clueless what to expect from one court date to the next. I had placed several calls to the administrator of DFCS with little to no response. The administrator who did communicate with me was replaced within a matter of weeks, and the new administrator lacked customer service skills. To date, he has yet to respond to any of my calls or concerns. DFCS changes staff and management more than a person changes underwear. No one was doing a thing to reunite my son with me, but I was relentless in my pursuit to get him back by whatever means necessary, within reason. I was tired of jumping through hoops for DFCS and CPS with no hope in sight of my son's return; at this point, I felt I had nothing to lose, so I had planned to just let it rip and let the chips fall wherever. DFCS was clueless as to what CPS was doing and vice versa. I was told that the two work independently, yet both were in court combating for the same child and against the same parent.

On May 5, 2006, I had to attend a mandatory meeting with the DFCS supervisor and a service called Family Ties to discuss wraparound services. The CPS caseworker, Ms. Recore, was also invited to this meeting, but I told the person in charge that if she was present, I would not attend. After all, this is the woman who showed my son's naked pictures to her colleagues at court and had verbally threatened to do all she could to land me in jail. I was told that Ms. Recore had suggested to them that I attend anger management, something she had been pushing since day one. I felt the meeting was a total waste of time. The services they offered were services I already had in place for my son and me, even before the child abuse accusations. I only requested to have a "buddy" or behavior aide sit with my son in school to assist with his behavioral challenges during school hours to avoid the school calling me at work throughout the day. I also requested the name and numbers of support groups or organizations for adoptive parents. Lastly, I requested a list of schools that my son could attend without fear of being kicked out because of his behavior, as well as ones that provided financial assistance getting him in. Of course, none of my requests were granted. There was really no other advice they could offer my son and I since all the pieces had already been in place. My attitude was borderline hostile as I thought of my time missed from work to discuss things already implemented, yet not seeming to be closer to reuniting with my son. As the meeting came to an end, I saw Ms. Recore sitting outside the door. I could hear them reporting to her the results of the meeting, and frankly I couldn't care less. I left and went home.

I called a mandatory meeting with the "powers that be" at Fulton DFCS. I was surprised that they agreed to the meeting, but then I guess they grew weary of my constant calls to administration and the governor's office. I had long since paid for a copy of the court transcript and submitted my concerns to the judge, along with a copy of the deprivation petition. With most of the children in DFCS custody being African American, I was shocked to learn that most of the staff at the meeting were also African American, except for the supervisor for CPS, Mr. Mudd, who was country Caucasian. There were more titles present than Carter's got liver pills or Kellogg's got Corn Flakes. So many titles, so many roles, yet oftentimes, the right hand did not know what the left hand was doing. There was the case-worker, the deputy director, program director, wraparound case-worker, social workers (two were present)… the list goes on with a total of eight people, all looking important in their suits but not one of them worth the paper this book is written on. Of course, the main person I wanted to see was not present, and this was the administrator for Fulton DFCS who felt he had better things to do than listen to a parent complain about not having her child with her. They all sat smiling politely, and I could tell that each of them already had a written mental script to run by me. I came prepared with a list of questions for DFCS. I wanted to know, for starters, why my son was taken to a destination unknown to me to be seen and tested by various psych and forensic specialists? Why was he questioned numerous times by various people to program and pollute his mind against his mother? Why was my son taken into custody without a thought about his health? He was sickly at our last visit. While in foster care, he lost weight, had two bruised knees, a lump on his forehead, a slight wheeze, and he complained of being nauseous and having two bloody noses, yet DFCS felt he was better off in foster care, not seen by a pediatrician… and I'm accused of child abuse? Are you *kidding* me? I wanted to know why Mr. Mudd had denied my son going home with his uncle and opted instead for foster care, especially since his uncle was present at the initial meeting and had provided all the information needed for a background check. Was this to be spiteful or what? Of course, Mr. Mudd stumbled through his answer to this question and never provided me with an answer. In fact, no one present had a decent answer to any of my questions which I knew would happen, but I got such a kick watching them squirm and look at each other as if trying to pull the answer from each other. Lastly, I wanted to know why my rights as a parent were violated but later learned that a parent accused of abuse has no rights. I was summoned to numerous meetings at the convenience of DFCS with no results and no closer to getting my son, and I demanded answers. I made it very clear to everyone present that I would do whatever it took to expose the corrupt system of DFCS and CPS to get my son back, and I left with newfound confidence despite going home alone again.

My son had a scheduled counseling session with our psychologist prior to the school drama with DFCS, and I requested his appointment be kept despite him being in state custody. I also demanded that I accompanied him to counseling. DFCS allowed the appointment, but this would be considered a visit rather than an appointment, meaning I couldn't expect an additional visit with my son. So, on May 7, 2006, I met the social worker with my son, and she followed me to our psychologist's office (my son wasn't even allowed to ride with me in the car to the doctor, a forty-minute ride). It was during our session that my son told our therapist that the older boy in foster care, whom I'll call Joey, called him a punk and got in the bed with him at night. He said, "Mommy, I don't even know what a punk is." Our doctor and I were both horrified. Of course, our doctor was very good at determining if any sexual abuse or molestation had taken place or was suspected. My son further stated how fearful he was of this older fifteen-year-old boy who was picking on him daily. As soon as the session was over, I told the social worker assigned to me what went on in our session regarding this other kid. I was very concerned that my son was going back to the same foster home as soon as we left the office of our therapist, despite my report. I felt he should have immediately been removed from the foster home. I went home and called every number I had, and if there was no answer, I left a detailed voice message. However, my son stayed in that foster home for at least another *two days*.

On May 9th, I went to court to meet with the judge, the CPS caseworker, Ms. Recore, and the SAAG to discuss the case plan. This was needed to get my son back expeditiously. Suddenly, there was a rush to get my son out of foster care and back to me. I'm sure that if it wasn't for the fact that they realized that his behavior was just as I had reported, and this new complaint arose of abuse in the foster home, they would have tried to place him in another foster home. However, the current foster parents were constantly complaining, the school that they had placed my son in was complaining, and, of course, I was complaining. The sorry attorney I had did not show up for this court appearance either; however, at this point, I had become an expert with court dealings and the DFCS jargon. The judge advised me that I could postpone until a time when my attorney could be present. I assured her that I was fine without my attorney. The one thing that the SAAG told the judge was that I had to comply with all the requests of the court. Basically, I had to agree to have a caseworker come to my home once a month, use no corporal punishment, and continue counseling. None of the interventions in the case plan were ideas suggested by DFCS or CPS. I was already receiving counseling for my son long before their involvement. I'd never been abusive to my son, and the only additional thing was having a caseworker come to my home once a month, which I welcomed—I had nothing to hide. The judge then asked me if I understood what I had to do in the following months, and I said I did. The great news was that my concerns regarding the deprivation petition were reviewed and it was thrown out of the court! I couldn't believe it! I finally scored a point. Thank you, Jesus! Ms. Recore of course, again suggested anger management because she was still trying to make her case stick that I was an out-of-control parent who really ought to be in jail. I told her frankly that she could go to anger management for me. At this point, I did not care. I was tired of kissing up and hoop jumping—just give me my son! Once the case plan was signed, I asked how soon I could pick him up, and unbelievably, Ms. Recore made me wait an additional day with no other reason than, I suspect, just to make me wait.

However, I was on cloud nine, and I felt certain I could wait another day; after all, they needed to make the paperwork look good in stating that they (DFCS and CPS) kept custody of my son for thirty days! Cha ching!

On May 10, 2006, my son and I ran into each other arms. It was also on May 10, 2006, that this Ms. Recore decided to give me a pamphlet titled "A Parent's Guide to a Child Protective Services (CPS) Investigation," something that should have been given to me at the very first meeting! I received it after my son was back with me, and I couldn't help thinking it was done intentionally. Here I had to stumble through the entire investigation, asking questions which were not answered, until I had received this pamphlet. Many of my questions were noted right in the pamphlet, which was probably why I had not received it—that would be too much like doing the right thing. It was even explained in the pamphlet about the thirty days for the caseworker to do an investigation; however, I was made to believe that the thirty days were due to the allegation, rather than the policy and procedure. Since communication is vital during any investigation, one would think that the CPS caseworker would foster the distribution of the information outlined in the pamphlet, especially if he or she is lacking in communication skills. However, perhaps her lack in communication skills was the reason for her incompetence; in any event, I was just glad and relieved to have my son back home. Our reunion was bittersweet as we embraced each other. I wondered what thoughts were running through his little brain as we stood in the DFCS office. To me, he looked like he had lost some more weight and was insecure in his mannerisms. All I wanted to do at that point was to get him home where he could feel comfort, security, and safety. I had nothing to say to Ms. Recore as I gathered my strength to walk out of the DFCS office. I don't even think I said thank you. I just wanted to get out into the warmth of the sun, with my son, and go home. I had planned a special dinner for us, and I took time off from work for us to bond once again. I felt like I was starting over with my son in fostering the mother/son relationship. He was very chatty, but he was careful not to discuss anything pertaining to the foster home he was in or the incident at the school and being carted away by CPS. I decided to allow him to discuss his experiences with me in his own time. Therefore, I was careful not to bring up anything unless he discussed it first. We ended our first day back together alone; we did not visit any family or friends, and at the end of the day, my son asked if he could sleep in my bed with me, I of course said *yes!*

CHAPTER 4. THE BONDAGE

"Stand fast therefore in the liberty wherewith Christ hath made us free, and be not entangled again with the yoke of bondage."
Galatians 5:1 KJV

I enrolled my son in a private school to keep both him and me from the embarrassment of nosy teachers and peers wondering what had happened. He had attended the school when he was in preschool, so it was good that he did not have to start over learning the teachers and the children in the small classroom setting. We both had had enough drama to last a lifetime, and all I wanted at that time was to bring some normalcy to our lives. It had been twenty-eight days since our reunion and departure from DFCS. I thought the day DFCS picked up my son from school was unforgettable; however, June 5, 2006, was to be a day I would never truly forget. The weather was beautiful—sunny with clear blue skies and not a rain cloud in sight. The temperature was oh so comfortable—not too hot and not too cold. I had dropped my son off to school and was about to go to work when I received a call which would forever change my life. Just when I thought I was climbing out of the pit, I fell headlong into an abyss of despair, gloom, and disbelief. This was a call that no one would ever want to receive. It was a call that makes your heart race to the point of spontaneous combustion, a call that dulls the mind and causes irregular breathing. That call makes you want to pinch yourself to assure you're not dreaming; it was surreal. The time was 8:00 a.m. when the phone rang. As I went to answer the phone, I sensed in my spirit that the call was not to be a pleasant call or courtesy call. It was a call from a Lieutenant Ford; there was a warrant out for my arrest, and he was demanding that I turn myself in to the police department. I'll never forget his words: "It'll go better for you if you turn yourself in." I asked what it was for, in utter shock, and his answer was cold and to the point. "For cruelty to children." I asked, Are you kidding me? and of course I knew he wasn't kidding about something so serious, but I couldn't believe that someone, anyone, would think me capable of such a heinous crime. I wanted to say, "Sir, you don't even know me. How dare you accuse me?" but what was the use? I managed only to ask where I need to show up and then hung up.

Since I didn't know how much time I had before a patrol car would pull up to my home, and to avoid the embarrassment in my neighborhood, I hid out in my studio until I was able to reach my new attorney. I called my brother in Christ who was as shocked as I was to hear this news just weeks after my son and I were reunited. Of course, no one cared about the welfare of my son, where I was to place him, or who would care for him while I was in jail. Here I was being jailed for cruelty to children, yet the very child I had allegedly abused was in my home with me, and neither DFCS nor CPS cared about his placement. I guess it was now okay for him to be with family. It wasn't enough to be dragged through the court, feeling humiliated and frustrated, missing time from work, missing money, and missing my son; it wasn't enough; just when I thought I had a breather in my life, I was to be carted off to jail. Guilty before innocent, charged before a court hearing, and never to see a judge or jury. I didn't even have an opportunity to speak with the police officer, and only the Lord knows what my initial whack attorney had to say to him. I kept telling myself that God did not give me this child to make my life a living hell. I had to keep reminding myself that God does not make mistakes, and the placement of my son with me was not a mistake. I kept telling myself that despite all the false accusations, finger-pointing, and whisperings in offices and gossip on phone lines, I was a good person, and the Lord knew exactly what I did and did not do. I kept telling myself that there was a reason for all this drama; even though I did not have the answer as to *why*, God was in control, and He had a plan and purpose for both my son and me.

I walked around my studio in the dark, praying and crying, crying and praying. One minute I was asking God what I did wrong, and the next I was calling the Devil a liar, knowing that I did nothing wrong. I was even afraid to turn on the studio light for fear of a patrol car pulling up to the door, and I had to rebuke this fear. I feared losing my freedom, and I had to rebuke the fear. I feared losing my son and perhaps my very life, and I had to rebuke these fears. I felt darkness all around me, and I was drowning in an abyss. I had to keep praying until I could feel the warmth of the Holy Spirit as He wrapped His arms around me and told me I was going to be okay. My heart was pounding. I felt nauseous and realized I hadn't eaten, but at that time I really did not feel like eating. It seemed like an eternity waiting for my attorney to call. My head was pounding, and I wasn't sure which was pounding the loudest—my heart or my head. My son was in school at the time, so at least I found a remedy for his safety while I was in jail. Thank God for the brother and sister He placed in my life that would be caring for my son during my brief incarceration. I was determined that I would not spend the night in jail. My studio felt cold, but the coolness felt good to my warm, dry skin. I felt dehydrated, but there was no water, and I dared not go outside to the store next door. I guess a part of me just wanted to die and be done with all the drama. I tried to do a good deed in my life, which was to share the good in my life with an unfortunate child. I've always loved children, and since I had none of my own, I wanted one to leave a legacy with. What little I had, I wanted to share with my child, but I did not want all the drama and life crises that are offered when dealing with a child through the system called DFCS. I tried to look halfway decent and fixed my hair up. I didn't feel like wearing any makeup; I tried to apply some but then thought how silly I was being. After all, a mug shot is a mug shot, and I'd never seen one look decent no matter how someone tried to dress.

The phone rang, and I nearly went through the roof. It was my attorney—a new one—who was very calming on the phone. We met, and he walked me through what I was about to deal with. I was surprised when he told me he would have to drive me to the police department. Of course he would; I just didn't think of having to go to jail in the first place. I left him with my house keys and cell phone. I walked into the police department and met with Lieutenant Ford, the same officer who, at the court, told my son not to admit that he "falls out," or he would go to jail. I already did not like this man. He was cold and asked my name, where I worked, my supervisor's name— things he already knew. I warned him not to call my job and speak to my supervisor, and I was equally cold. At this point, I didn't care. I was already being arrested, so what more could he do? He said it was just for verification, but I didn't believe a word he had to say. My attorney had a sidebar with him, and I saw the pictures of my son that the lieutenant had blown up with a colored hue, which made the pictures look far worse than the pictures shown to us by Child Protective Services. The whole picture was an orange color. He then called in a female officer who *placed hand cuffs on me!* I looked at her in horror and asked if it was really necessary. She told me it was the law and that she had to cuff me, but she would not tighten the cuffs (as if this would make me feel better). The handcuffs felt cold and heavy to my tiny wrists and were totally uncomfortable. This was the kind of stuff I saw on *C.S.I.*, *N.C.I.S.*, or *Law and Order*, but never in my wildest nightmare did I ever think it would be a reality in my life. The lieutenant's goal was to make me spend a few nights in jail, which was part of a conversation I had overheard between him and whoever was on the other end of the phone. I said to myself, "The Devil is a liar, and I will not spend one night in jail." I reminded the Lord that I did not have the anointing of Paul and Silas to stay in jail singing praise songs (as if the Lord needed to know this). Further, the lieutenant wanted me carted to downtown Fulton County Jail, knowing full well that if I ended up at Fulton, it just may be days before I was released; it takes forever to appear before a judge there, and I guess this is why he felt so sure that I would be in jail for a while. However, the lieutenant did not know the relationship I had with the Almighty Judge, and for some reason, I was driven to a smaller jail just outside the city limits, literally minutes from my home. Still, I overheard the lieutenant say that he would fax the paperwork needed to transfer me from the smaller jail to Fulton County Jail. At this point, I did not worry, fully confident that my God would not allow this to happen.

When I arrived at the jail, the staff there took one look at me and said, "You don't even belong here." I totally agreed. I had the favor of God in that they did not make me strip or put on an orange suit. In fact, they were very comforting, saying, "You won't be here long. Your attorney will get you out shortly." I was placed in a holding cell, which was a metal cage similar to what you would put your dog in at home. I took a hard swallow before walking inside that cage totally alone and then I was asked to turn around so the cuffs could be removed. It was a cage just big enough for a human or two with one, single metal bench in the middle of it. I sat down feeling the coldness of the bench through my pants, and no matter how long I sat, there was no warming of that bench. I don't know how Paul and Silas did it, but there were no praise songs coming out of me at that time. All I could think about was how much I hated that Lieutenant Ford and the teacher who had called DFCS in the first place. The temperature in the cage was surprisingly comfortable despite the cold bench. My nose was stuffy from all the crying at my studio, so

I couldn't smell a thing, but my surroundings were very clean. As I looked through the bars, there was an area directly across from me set up like a hospital's nursing station, and this is where the officers processed their paperwork. After about twenty minutes, an officer came over to let me out for the mug shot. For some reason, I thought of the actor Nick Nolte when he took that hideous mug shot years ago. I was prepared to hold up a numbers sign but was told I didn't have to do all that, that I was just to stand there, and within seconds, it was over. I really must commend the staff at the jail who sensed my pain and were trying to make the process as painless as possible. Of course, there is always one butthead in the group who spoke roughly to me while returning me to the cage, but for some reason I was undaunted, I guess because I was so numb.

There was a clock on the wall, and I quickly learned that by watching the time, it only prolonged the waiting. I had arrived at the jail at 10:00 a.m., and it was now noon, but it already seemed like I'd been in the cage for much longer. The phone rang, and when the officer got off the phone, he told me that it was Lieutenant Ford who wanted to know if I had been transferred to Fulton County Jail. I guess he saw the fear in my eyes (after all, years ago I was the Director of Nursing at Fulton County Jail); he told me not to worry because the paperwork was never received, and no one knew where it was. He further stated that without that paperwork, I would be staying right where I was until my attorney could get me out. I thanked God, and I thanked him. As for my attorney, he stopped by to ask if I had any collateral to put up for bond; all I had was my home. I was surprised at this questioning because he was supposed to have been working on my case since dropping me off at the jail; however, I learned he had other things to do, and he was waiting for this or that. I really didn't understand a thing he was saying. For all I knew, it was just a bunch of excuses, and I remember snapping at him just to get me out! He seemed to understand how I was feeling and was patient, despite my impatience; he was cool, calm, and collected, something that concerned me. I felt that if my attorney didn't have the same urgency as I did to get me out of jail, then I would be in for a long night, but at that point, beggars couldn't be choosers, and he knew this. I was stuck with him.

I watched as the officers processed more inmates, about ten men all in orange jumpsuits. They came in with shackles on their feet, which were removed so that each one could get their picture taken. They all seemed to be in a good mood for some reason. I remember feeling totally uncomfortable as they all stared at me like I was a caged piece of meat. I guess to them I was. I looked down quickly, not wanting to make eye contact with any of them. I turned my back to them as best I could, which felt kind of awkward but not as awkward as having a group of strange men gawking at me. I was so glad when their processing was over, and they were taken to the "real jail cells" in back. For a small jail, it was quite busy as the evening grew near. It was 5:00 p.m., and I had not heard a thing. Even the officers said, "Damn. I thought your attorney would have had you out by now." So did I. They offered me dinner, but I wasn't hungry, and the last thing I wanted was jail food. I'm sure it may have been good, but I guess I'd watched too much TV, and I really didn't want to find out the truth about jail food one way or another. I could smell the food as the trays were distributed just behind my cage and through another door, and it smelled pretty good, but I wasn't eating. I thought about what my son was doing at that moment, wondering if he had been told that his mother was in jail, but I took comfort in knowing that he was with family, and therefore, he was just fine. I thought about Ms. Recore and her comment at the court, "She's gon' to jail," with her no-talking self. Mainly, I thought about God and His plan and purpose for this incarceration. Perhaps I'd never understand the reason for all that, but I know that if I was to survive it, I needed to keep a cool head on my shoulder, grab on to my peace, and not waver in my faith. I very briefly thought of calling my church, but I knew well that I would never get through to speak with my pastor, no matter how many years I'd been a member. If I spilled my guts on the phone, I may have gotten his third-in-command, but by the next day, the news would be all over the church. *I'll pass*, I thought. By 8:00 p.m., my butt was tender, and my lower back was telling me my age. I stood up in my cage and stretched as best I could and then sat back down on the cold bench. The staff had already changed shifts around 7:00 p.m., and I remember hearing the oncoming shift ask the staff leaving why my attorney hadn't gotten me out yet, something I was also wondering. Since his visit at noon, I hadn't seen or heard from him, and I was so disappointed and devastated. I needed to walk, and I remember I had not been to the bathroom. I was hoping to have been out of jail to use my own bathroom, but I realized that it wasn't happening anytime soon, so I asked permission to go to the restroom and was escorted by a male officer. I remember, while walking to the bathroom, praying that he wouldn't have to go inside with me. He didn't, but once inside, I looked around for the hidden cameras (I remembered seeing on TV that there were hidden cameras in the jails where the toilets are). Have you ever tried to pee without showing your tail? My urinating was so camouflaged that if they had cameras, they would have a very hard time seeing my gifts! The short walk to and from the restroom was unusually refreshing, but the step back into the cage was a harsh reality. I felt like I had worked a twelve-hour shift just from sitting in that cage all day. As I sat on that bench, I had to get use to the coldness of the metal all over again. It was 10:00 p.m., and an officer said to me, "Listen, we don't know what happened to your attorney. Why don't you just call the bail bondsmen? There's one right down the street, and we work with her all the time. You'll be out before you know it. Is there a family member you can call for the cash?" I thought it looked like a job I better handle for myself, so I called my brother who made all the arrangements, but he was short on some of the cash and called me back. I then called my best friend to ask her for the difference. She didn't have the cash, but thank God the bail bondsman accepted credit cards. One hour later, I was sprung! I never heard from my attorney until I called to say I was out (no thanks to him), I had to remind him that he had my car key, house key, and cell phone, items I had to give him prior to being put in jail.

It was midnight when I arrived home with my son. All I did was hold him close to me, speaking no words, at least not right away. I put on his pajamas, and he hopped into my bed. Of course, he wanted to know where I was and why I did not pick him up from school, and, with the help of the Holy Spirit, I told him in a way that a child would understand. I explained to him what it was like for mommy to be in jail. Most importantly, I explained the need for him to be obedient and not "fall out" hurting himself or hit adults, explaining to him the potential consequences of his behaviors. I then took a very long hot shower, allowing the heat of the water to warm my body from the cold metal I had felt in the cage. I wanted to wash away all thoughts of DFCS, CPS, the police department, and the jail. I wanted to wash away the nightmare that had haunted me since April 10, 2006. The shower felt good, and I spent most of my time in it thanking the Lord for deliverance. I couldn't believe how sweet it was to be sprung and how I had wasted the entire day waiting for my attorney who never did respond back. I was so angry at him, but I had to be cool because I was still dependent on him for the upcoming court appearance. After my shower, I had a nice soothing cup of tea, and I closed my eyes as I felt the hot liquid warming the inside of my body. It felt so good going down, and I appreciated a simple cup of tea so much while sitting up in my own bed. I tried to clear my mind just for the short time it took for me to finish my tea; however, my thoughts kept reminding me that I had actually been in a jail cage which to me seemed more uncomfortable than an actual jail cell. I thanked God that my destination was not a jail cell. I had finished my tea, and I lay down beside my son who was sound asleep. I pulled him closer to me and just held him and whispered, "Boy, you better know that I love you unconditionally—what a mother won't do for her child." I then thanked God for getting me through that day, and I prayed for healing in my back which was still in quite a bit of pain because the Advil I had taken wasn't helping just yet. Somehow I fell fast asleep with thoughts of that cold metal bench, a cage, and loss of freedom. That bench never got warm!

The alarm went off the following morning, and as I got out of the bed to get ready for work and to send my son off to school, my body reminded me that I was no longer a young teenager. I really did not feel like going to work; however, I didn't feel like staying at home alone. I didn't feel like thinking up a creative excuse for not reporting to work, and I needed to make money because I now had an attorney to pay (not that the services were worth it so far). I got my son up for school, trying as best I could to proceed as normal in my home life. As unusual and abnormal our lives had become, I didn't want my son to feel the backlash from being taken from his mother, placed in a foster home, returned to his mother, only to then be separated again, picked up from school by his uncle, united back with his mother, and then to resume his education in yet another school. There was no way I could return my son to the school that had called DFCS and had him carted away in the middle of the school day with no notice to his mother. Thank God for the private school I had started him in for preschool and the teacher who was willing to work with me finan-cially. His private teacher has since gone to be with the Lord, but I shall never forget her kindness in helping me with my son.

I no sooner got to work than I realized that I had made a mis-take and perhaps should have stayed at home. It was hard keeping my mind on my patients and workload and not to digress to the night before when I was caged like an animal. As I sat at my desk, my area of tenderness reminded me of the cold hard metal bench I sat on for hours, waiting to hear from an attorney who never responded back to me. When I took my break to go to the restroom, I was reminded of the freedom I had in that I did not have to ask permission to use the restroom. I smiled at work and tried to maintain an outward display of joy; however, my insides were a bunch of nerves, anger, sadness, and dismay at the whole legal system. My mind kept drifting back to the nightmare of the day before, from the time the lieutenant called me until I walked out of my cage near midnight. I thought, *Is all this even necessary, and is the law set up to punish suspects even before a verdict is rendered?* My entire life was on the verge of being destroyed because I dared to step out and do what so many others have had the ability to do but chose not to, and that is to adopt a child who originally belonged to someone else, a child who was not of their blood but certainly, in time, would become a part of their spirit. My day at work was a long day. I tried to stay as busy as possible which wasn't hard to do at my place of employment. Somehow, I managed to keep my mind on my work for most of the day. I did not disclose to my manager any events of the previous day; however, at the end of my day, I did confide in my supervisor who was a born-again Christian. Many times, we had met in her office for prayer, sometimes for her and sometimes for me. On that day, the prayer was for me, and she knew all too well the inner turmoil I was enduring and the appreciation for a prayer of agreement.

CHAPTER 5. THE STRONGHOLD

"For the weapons of our warfare are not carnal but mighty through God to the pulling down of strong holds."
2 Corinthians 10:4 KJV

Life teaches you that things are not always as they appear to be, and if something is too good to be true, it most often is. Having said that, once I had received my get-out-of-jail card (being facetious), I was told by my attorney that it was all over. When I asked about court, I was told that it would be a while before I had to appear in court, if I had to appear at all, because it may get thrown out of court, thus closing the case. I thought that would be wonderful, but from what I'd learned of our legal system, DFCS, CPS, I wasn't holding my breath for this to happen to me. There'd just been too many issues to consider and too much baggage to carry.

The biggest problem with our system regarding child abuse is that DFCS, CPS, and the police department each run their own separate investigations. This wouldn't be so bad if, in the end, they all came together to compare notes, but unfortunately, they do not. So even if DFCS clears you of any charges, you still have to contend with CPS and the police department. Even crazier is that DFCS and CPS can both close your case, but you still have to deal with the police department that was called in the first place by DFCS and/or the school. I was told that it's the law that the police have to be called once DFCS is contacted for a case of abuse; however, it's at the police's discretion to prosecute. So, you go through juvenile court which closes or dismisses your case, and just when you think you can resume your life and get back to normal, you learn that you have to not only go to jail, but go through superior court to fight for your freedom, *even though your allegedly abused child still lives with you!* None of these organizations communicates your case with each other, so they can all be on the same page, nor do they care to know what the other is doing or has done. My anger at this system is greatest toward the tiny police department who had nothing better to do than prosecute a single woman who was trying to make a better life for a misfortunate child. My battle with DFCS was more or less an open-and-shut case, but dealing with the police lieutenant and superior court took three long years to conclude. Actually, once the lieutenant turned in his report, he was free to live his life normally; however, I was the one going through years of hell, in and out of superior court waiting for a trial that may never happen.

As the days progressed, my son continued to exhibit inappropriate and hostile behaviors both in school and in church. I felt like I was starting all over with him concerning his behaviors, no thanks to DFCS, CPS, and the police. With the behaviors came a recurrence of episodes of anxiety separation. He still had periods of "falling out" and thrashing about on the floor, banging his head and arms when he could not have his way, but the frequency of this self-abusive behavior had greatly decreased. I think, if nothing else, being involved with DFCS, CPS, and the law had scared the hell out of my son, which may have been the reason for the decrease in episodes. I had to start all over reassuring my son that I was not going to leave him. As I said the words to him, in my mind I doubted myself, not knowing what the law had in store for me and lacking all confidence in the justice system. I was sincerely hoping that I truly did not have to leave him again. However, the last time I had uttered words about never leaving my son, he was briefly taken from me by DFCS to a foster home. Shortly after his return to me, I was taken to jail, and his uncle ended up picking him up from school, and we were separated again. It would be a challenge convincing my son that Momma was not going anywhere, but first I had to convince myself.

For days, months, and years, I lived my life under a black cloud, not knowing when I was to report to court and start the process all over again in a different court. The case had been closed by DFCS and the deprivation petition thrown out of juvenile court, but thanks to the staff at the school who called the police, I now had to deal with the superior court. This was a nightmare that did not want to end, a stronghold that did not want to let go. For something to be so common sense in nature, the courts were bringing the case to a whole new and different level. It seemed to be common sense that if the Department of Family and Children Services, along with Child Protective Services, had closed the case, and the judge reviewed the deprivation petition and ruled that it be "vacated" or thrown out of court, then there should not even be a case in superior court, regardless of their independence of each other. However, something like that can only be resolved through prayer and fasting. I lived hopefully from day to day, still dealing with the issues that surrounded charges in the first place, still dealing with a son who had special needs, still dealing with the ridicule of people who knew nothing and had nothing to do with our case, and still just dealing. To add insult to injury, I was accused of criminal charges, cruelty to children and child abuse, such a heinous crime. While all the accusations were going on, my son was still in my care without any help or supervision from any Child Protective Services. I was an alleged criminal who was facing criminal charges, yet the law cared so little for this child that they were okay to have this innocent child live with the alleged criminal. Each time my son had an episode in school when he had injured another child or even himself, or he was suspended from school because of fighting his teachers, I was reminded of my ordeal with DFCS and CPS, and I wondered where the court was when I was going through this silent hell with my son, where the justice for the parent was or support for the single parent who was never told of this child's history in the first place. Had I had the opportunity to know all the facts before making the decision to adopt this child, matters would have been different and perhaps better. However, I have to tell myself more that God is in control, and He does not make mistakes. My son is with me for a reason, and I've had to go through this mess for a reason.

Almost a whole year passed before I received any information about a court date, and when it came in the mail, it was like a knife slash to the jugular. I was so surprised, hurt, and angry by the demand to appear in court for criminal charges. To make matters worse, when I called my attorney to inquire about the court date, he was not even aware of it. However, there was a bit of hope in his not knowing, so I thought. My thinking was that if my attorney did not know about the court date, perhaps someone had made a mistake, and there was no date. The mistake was in my attorney's failure to keep informed about my case. I couldn't believe that after a whole year of my son living with me that the law still wanted to pursue criminal charges against me. It was a system that was so dysfunctional to allow a child to reside with an alleged criminal parent yet be allowed to judge that same parent in a court of law, and it was absurd yet a fact here in the United States of America. I wondered how many other innocent parents were out there being lynched by the law because of an over-reacting teacher, relative, or enemy who decided to call DFCS or CPS which led to a call to the police.

Please don't misunderstand me, I know for a fact that there are children who are being abused by their parents or loved ones; however, there are clearly multiple signs and symptoms which denote child abuse, which goes far deeper than a bruise on a wrist, such as multiple bruising, scratches or areas of swelling, evidence of old wounds, fractures, or even broken bones. Far deeper are the emotional scars in the child who has suffered abuse, yet these scars are also invisible and overlooked. Areas to explore are like how the child responds to a parent, or a history of unexplained bruises or marks on the child, and so on. One would expect the experts to know these things and further investigate, searching deeper than just superficial scars or marks, keeping in mind the impact on the child should he/she be permanently or temporarily removed from the parent. Teachers, just like nurses working in the emergency room, need to learn what true child abuse is all about and not be so quick to jump the gun and call DFCS at the first sign of a bruise, especially in a child about whom the teacher has called the parent numerous times with complaints of hostility and self-abuse. I've held meetings with his teachers, principal, assistant principal, and the school psychologist, and everyone was aware of my son's behavior, but no one at his school wanted to help me deal with it. I guess their remedy was to assume I was a bad parent, and by calling DFCS, this would remove both me and my son from the school. The dirty part was that once the school called DFCS, who came and carted my son out of the school around 2:15 p.m., the good-for-nothing school principal didn't even bother to call me until almost 5:30 p.m., when I was on my way to the school's afterschool program to pick up my son.

It seems that the law, while trying to protect our children, has made it all too easy to report abuse, regardless of if it is valid or not. Anyone can literally pick up a phone and call anonymously, which sets the wheels in motion like a SWAT team. People making these calls rarely think of the impact on the child, regardless if the charge is valid or not. There is no thought of the aftereffects on both the parent and the child. Unless you have been inside the workings of DFCS and CPS, you are clueless as to just how much protecting these children have rendered to them. In my experience, my son was traumatized more by all the questioning of strangers and being made to strip with all those strange people looking at his naked body and private area. He remembered that his pediatrician and I had told him that no one is to see his private area, except Mommy and the doctor, and he's to tell Mommy if anyone else had or tried to. I found myself trying to explain to my son why all these people were looking at his naked-ness. Then there was the brain washing—putting words in his mouth like "Don't your mommy beat you when you act up?" or, "What does your mommy use to hit you with?" These were questions to entrap the child into saying just what they wanted to hear for them to twist and present in a court of law. After all the questioning and examin-ing, the child was taken by strangers to an even stranger place called a foster home. Only God knows the answers he was given when he asked about where his mommy was or why he couldn't go home. Thank God my son only stayed in a foster home for a few weeks due to a fighting parent who kept *all* her documentation.

After a year or so I had to go to court. Missing time from work and not knowing what to expect, I looked up the directions to the court on MapQuest and called my brother to make sure he was going to be there with me. I arrived at the court and waited for hours for the judge to appear. They make you show up for court hours before the judge is actually ready to hear your case. My mouth was dry, and I was angry at even being summoned to court on bogus charges. To add insult to injury, my attorney wasn't very comforting and communica-tive. I had a million thoughts and twenty questions I wanted to ask, but all he could say was that it was "normal procedure." There was nothing normal about what I was going through. When the judge finally showed up, there was the forever-long roll call of everyone on the court calendar. When your name was called, you stood up, and if you had an attorney, he/she would stand with you, along with the prosecutor. When my name was called, we all stood up; however, the ADA (Assistant District Attorney) advised the judge that he did not have time to review my case due to a murder case he was working on, so I was rescheduled. My attorney explained to me that I would get another date for court to try the case. I was angry; I had wasted four hours of work to sit in a court for nothing, only to turn around and go back to work for the remainder of the day. This mess continued for *three long years*. I would get summoned to court, lose time from work, burn up gas driving to downtown Atlanta, spend money I couldn't afford for parking, only to turn around and leave the court not having been tried or heard by the judge because the case was with yet another ADA who did not have the time to review the case. In total, my case has been in the hands of at least five ADA's by my last count. While the court and the judge kept putting me on a back burner, my career was spiraling downhill. I've been to court so many times I've lost count, but I have a stack of summons sent in the mail for each court appearance. While I was being inconvenienced by court appearances, the police lieutenant who pressed charges in the first place was proceeding as usual with his life and daily work, not even remembering me or what he had done to me and my son. He didn't even have to appear in the court. Imagine that!

For three years, I lived my life feeling like there was a black cloud over my head, a stronghold. I never knew what to expect or when the next shoe would fall. The legal system is so messed up that I even had people calling my home stating they were the Victim Advocate for my son and wanted to know when the next DFCS court date was, so they could be present to represent my son and walk me through the process. They were so misinformed that not only did they not know that the case was closed, but they thought they were calling the foster home! I had received at least five of these calls within the first year after the case was thrown out of juvenile court. Each time they called, they would leave an urgent message on my voice mail stating the need for me to call them back, and to me this was totally unbelievable. Now remember, my son was supposed to be protected by these people who didn't even know where he was staying and confusing his residence. I must admit I was amused at one of the woman's expressions when she learned that she was speaking with the mother, and my son was residing with me. I remember her response on the phone was, "Oh my, so the child is back with you?" to which I replied that he had been with me for over six months since the court date or nine months since the court date. It amazed me that I kept getting the same calls from the Victim-Witness Assistance Program (VWAP) which is the formal name for this program which hails from the district attorney's office. The services they offered were counseling and helping you get through the process of court which sounded great; unfortunately, these services were only available to the victim which was my son, and assuming he was in a foster home, I kept getting the calls; however, they eventually learned that I was indeed the accused parent, and the child was with me and the case was closed, and the calls abruptly ended. I felt like the victim, but there were no kind of services available to the parent who's been accused of abuse, no counseling services or preparation for courts; all this was left to the attorney I hired to represent me, and one must pray to God that the attorney is like the ones I've only seen on TV who take your hand and are constantly keeping you informed about your case. This was the type of attorney who meets with you the night before your court date or calls you the night before to explain what to expect or just to see if you're okay emotionally. I was glad to see my attorney showed up because there were times when he was running late, and I thought I would have to represent myself. Clearly, bedside manners were lacking now; somehow he had changed from when I first met him. However, I did not care as long as he represented me appropriately. I thought of patients who, when faced with a terminal illness, don't care if their cardiologist lacks bedside manners if he's known to be the best there is. So it was with me, but I wasn't so lucky. My attorney may be knowledgeable about his profession, but I did not see the full demonstration of this in his practice. I'm sure he tried his best, but he did not do much to expedite my case, and most of the people I've spoken with who work in the legal system concurred. There were many not so professional comments made about my attorney, and some were by his peers.

CHAPTER 6. THE BEGINNING

**"Though your beginning was small,
yet your latter end would greatly increase."
Job 8:7 KJV**

It had been three long years, and I was still dealing with the issues resulting from a defective legal system. Since being falsely accused of child abuse or cruelty to children, I've lost my job and been unemployed for over seven months, I now have a record, my career has been ruined, not to mention my reputation, and I'm behind in all my utilities, my car payments, and my mortgage. My so-called best friends have ceased communicating with me, but then I guess they never really were friends in the first place. I no longer have an attorney and must place my chances with a court-appointed attorney, but this may be a blessing in disguise provided the public defender's office ever return my numerous calls. My son is now on medication, which I'm closely monitoring because sometimes I think it's working, and other times I'm not so sure. I feel like I've practically been on staff at his school, but without the benefits of a paycheck. To add insult to injury, it was Christmas time, and I had no idea where I was going to get money for my son's gifts, food, and, at that point, even my shelter was on the line. Our Thanksgiving was a blessing in that my sister funded our drive to Virginia to spend it with her. But I missed the holiday atmosphere in my home where I would cook a full dinner for my son and me; However, I had no money for food, and all the food pantries were empty thanks to our weakened economy. In the past, we would watch the Macy's parade while pigging out on coffee cake, milk for him, and coffee for me. For the first time in my life with my son, I suffered from severe lack, and it was also the first for him. I pulled him from the afterschool enrichment program because I could no longer afford it, and we both missed this. I felt like Job who lost everything, and although I'd not lost everything yet, the challenges had certainly been as severe as Job's but in modern times.

I went to DFCS to apply for food stamps on November 5, 2008, so my son and I could have a decent Thanksgiving; however, despite my calls to determine the status of my request, no one from DFCS notified me until well after Thanksgiving. In fact, my call came December 1st, saying, "denied." The reason was because I received unemployment and adoption assist, which didn't cover half the bills, let alone food. The little checks I received were divided up among utilities, so I could have the electric needed for my son's breathing treatments at night, water to at least keep clean and cook whatever food I did have, and a phone in case of emergencies, God forbid. This still did not include my car payment and mortgage. However, DFCS felt I did not need food stamps, and to add insult to injury, I wasn't even advised of the procedure to appeal or if I could appeal. The caseworkers call was short and to the point, "Ms. Carter, you've been denied for food stamps, but I put your name in for some toys for your son." Toys?!? We needed food! The sad thing was that that caseworker really felt like she was doing me a favor requesting toys when we actually needed food, but that's DFCS for you, always backward ass (pardon the expression). My call to the supervisor to dispute the decision regarding my food stamps went unanswered, and the voice messages were not returned, so I decided to make a personal visit. I arrived at the DFCS office on Stonewall Tel to find it slightly crowded. The receptionist told me I had to fill out a communication form just to speak with the supervisor. After I completed this form, the receptionist would input the information into the system, and the person I wished to speak with hopefully would be sitting at her desk to see the message on her computer; if not, I would just be sitting in the waiting room until she did, and that is what I had to do. Finally, the supervisor came from the back room to speak with me, and it was at that time she told me that all I had to do was write a letter requesting an appeal and give it to her. I sat in the waiting room for twenty minutes for a five-minute conversation. I thanked her and left. I went upstairs to my post-adoption caseworker and had her type a quick letter for me which I signed and took back downstairs; I refused to go back home and then drive back to DFCS. I had to complete another communication form, and I waited another twenty minutes before I saw the same supervisor coming to the window to ask the receptionist a question, and I interrupted her. She looked surprised to see me so soon as I placed my letter in her hands and told her to have a blessed day and abruptly left. I was angry that it took *an hour and thirty minutes* for a twenty-minute process (which was getting the letter typed), all of which could have been avoided had the supervisor returned my call in the first place.

Weeks later, I received my court date to appeal for food stamps, on January 15, 2009, three months after my original request. I was hoping that by then I would not even need food stamps. I later learned that the appeal process was just another way the federal government attempts to cover their butts to keep from being sued for violating anyone's rights. They allow you to appeal, which means they'll listen to why you feel you qualify for food stamps, but they won't comply or change their decision. When I asked the judge why they would even send me a notice to appeal, the judge himself told me, "I can hear what you have to say, but I can't change anything. It's the policy of the federal government, not me." While we were waiting for the judge, one of the social workers shared with a brother, who was also there to appeal for food stamps, that we were wasting our time. He stated that they (meaning the court) have never changed the decisions of the social workers. When I asked him what the purpose of the court was, he said it was just to make sure the social workers had dotted the I's and crossed the T's. I remember thinking how I hoped this social worker was wrong or just exaggerating; unfortunately, he was absolutely correct. I further learned that they qualify you by what your *gross* unemployment earnings are, not the net. I tried to argue that I was not getting the gross in my pocket (over one hundred dollars were taken out for taxes before I got a dime), and I missed the qualifying amount by *two dollars and sixty-three cents!* I watched as social workers paraded into the courtroom with their manila folders, smiling at us fools sitting there to argue a lost cause. They already knew the answers even before we stepped in front of the judge. I watched as case after case was refused food stamps, each case being heard in less than ten minutes. So, when it was my time to be heard, I was not surprised by the verdict. So once again, I drove thirty miles to yet another court, wasted time and gas and paid another five dollars I couldn't afford for parking, walked two blocks in downtown Atlanta, in the cold, to get to the court, only to be denied food stamps for my son and I because I received two dollars and sixty-three cents over the allotted amount (which is bull since the feds are basing it on gross amount).

In hindsight and to keep myself from becoming depressed, I looked at my situation from God's perspective. I saw that I would not be a good witness for my Lord stating that God would supply all my needs while shoving a public assist food stamp in the hands of a cashier. I could hear God asking me if, so far during my time of unemployment, did I lacked any food? Of course, my son and I always had something to eat. The Word of God says, "I have been young, and now old; yet have I not seen the righteous forsaken, nor his seed begging bread" (Psalms 37:25 KJV). We may not have had steak or lobster, but we ate well and ate to the full, and I had to repent for my complaining about not having food stamps. So even in my short period of disappointment, I'm eternally grateful for the many blessings God had already bestowed on my son and me, and in the end, I had to painfully admit that I really did not need food stamps as long as I continued to keep God as my source.

On another given day, I called my electric company to see if they would work with me regarding my bill which, despite my fifty dollars here and there, was still a little over $500! It was winter and although I'd placed storm windows and door stoppers to keep out the cold, houses built now are less than adequate when it comes to heating. My humble abode was still chilly on cold days, and my thermostat was never over seventy-four degrees, but the house felt like the low fifties at times. When the supervisor told me she could not help me and that my services would be terminated despite my special needs son, I asked her what services pays them for people in situations as I. She then looked on one of their customers' bills and told me of a community outreach that helps with the utilities and provided me with a phone number. I called the number and was told I needed to be at the DFCS office on Stonewall Tel on Tuesday (which was the next day) by 9:00 a.m. and that they would be there from 11:00 a.m. to 4:00 p.m.; however, to beat the crowd I was told I should arrive early as they only service sixty-five people. I thanked her and hung up. I then called my post adoption caseworker who was in the same building where this service was being provided to see if she knew of this service as I had gone to her for help also. She was not aware of this service, which I thought was shameful since her role was to aid parents of adoption. I provided her with all the information I had, so she could be of service to others in my position going forward. I arrived at DFCS the next day by 8:00 a.m.; however, when I arrived, I was told that they had already met their quota. In fact, the officer there told me they had a near riot because one lady jumped in front of another. I was so disappointed and once again felt hopeless, but just for a minute. I went upstairs to my caseworker and told her what had happened and requested to use her phone. I called the community service again and asked if they had any other locations they serviced, and she provided me a list for them; however, at that time, any other place would also be packed and would have met their quota. I had no other choice but to wait until the following Tuesday. However, I decided to go to the DFCS office located on Fairburn Road instead.

The following Tuesday was a cold, rainy day. I woke wishing I could just stay in bed and sleep as my back and right leg were painful (a challenge resulting from an auto accident years ago). On cold or rainy days, the pain was more intense, and, on that day, I had both the cold and the rain. However, I was determined to get some help, any kind of help, for my son and me. I arrived at the DFCS on Fairburn at 7:45 a.m. and saw the line of umbrellas outside the building. *Oh Lord*, I thought, *couldn't you have given me sunshine?* I grabbed my umbrella and joined the line praying that I was within the sixty-five quotas. Just standing in line was comical, and although I had to stand in the cold and rain, I was entertained while doing so. The first thing I noticed in line was the smell of pure grain alcohol, which was nauseating. In front of the two ladies ahead of me stood a woman who looked well over sixty-five years old; however, this service was not for anyone sixty-five or over as they were serviced the previous month. She was about five feet three inches tall and maybe eighty-nine pounds with the jeans and jacket on. She had big gray and black sponge rollers in her gray hair and looked like a hot mess. It was obvious that she was still inebriated, and when she turned around in the line and told us she was going to cook some chicken for those standing in the line but had overslept, she confirmed her alcohol content was still a bit over the limit. In addition to this, she had a stack of papers (bills) which she kept dropping on the wet pavement in the rain. This service was only for electric bills, so there was no reason for a bunch of other bills. She was pleasantly tipsy and very talkative; it was only her odor of alcohol that was very offensive first thing in the morning. I'm not sure who looked the worst, her or her buddy, who was just the opposite. She was a tall woman weighing about 250 pounds or more. What tickled me about her was that among her many missing teeth, she had one large tooth in the front of her upper gum and was in line stating, "I'm not gon' to the dentist today coz it's raining," as she chomped away on a candy cane like it was a three-course meal. Then she proceeded to talk about a local politician who had AIDS and what he did and who he did it with. I couldn't hear the name, but apparently, he was someone everyone standing in the line with her knew, and I quite frankly didn't want to know his name. I felt like I had enough issues of my own than to get involved in idle gossip. No one standing in that line had authority to talk about anyone else because none of us were any better. We all had different circumstances, but we all had the same need on this particular day, time, and line, and that was help paying the electric bill!

Next, I was a bit alarmed by the constant yelling and arguing among the people at the front of the line. Apparently, two young girls who looked to be about eighteen years old were in line behind me eating chicken. They saw a friend of theirs up front and attempted to jump the line. This sent a frenzy of profanities, yelling, and total drama. To make matters worse, they refused to move despite a near beatdown from twenty other people. This later delayed the community outreach staff from servicing us with the needed numbers to receive help with the electricity. The staff kept yelling for the people to move back and stop crowding the door, but no one was moving for fear of these girls or someone else jumping in front. There was a chubby security guard who was useless, stating he was there for DFCS only and had nothing to do with the organization servicing the community. He was too ignorant to realize that the organization was on DFCS property, and he still had a job to do. One of the volunteers for the organization was a young girl around twenty-three with tight pants and a low-cut blouse who came outside and started yelling at us to move back or we'd get nothing. She further stated that the police were being called and we could either deal with the staff and move back or deal with the police and go to jail. When no one paid her any attention, despite her shaking and twitching, she yelled to another volunteer to just forget it, stating, "We're not giving them anything," as if the money was coming out of her pocket, and she went back inside the building. I could understand her trying to get the crowd organized, but her ghetto fabulous ways were not the key to achieving that. It got so bad with the yelling, cussing, and no one moving back so the staff could do their job, that the police had to be called. I was so relieved when they finally arrived, and so were many others because as soon as the people saw the police, they started clapping. Finally, there was some organization, and another volunteer started passing out numbers until they reached the number sixty-five. I was so thrilled to get number sixty; it was so wonderful, and I profusely thanked God. I had been standing in the rain for almost two hours, and my feet were ice cold inside of my socks. It was still raining but not as hard as earlier. I was surprised to see that despite the heavy rains, I was mostly dry—thank God for the small things. After receiving the numbers, we were told that we would have to come back by 1:30 p.m. to be processed. *Oh boy*, I thought, *still another step to go through*. We still had to sign our names by the assigned numbers and return in order to receive the help. I had just enough time to go home, take an hour-long nap, and go pick up my son from school in order to be back by 1:30 p.m. Although his school was not over until 2:20 p.m., there was no way I would be back from DFCS before his school was out, so unfortunately, he would have to be with me. I got back to my car thanking God first of all that I still had my car, and I turned the heat on my feet full blast.

Although I had not eaten breakfast or anything, when I arrived home from DFCS, I was too tired to eat, so I set the clock for an hour and took a nap. I later woke and went to the school to get my son, so I would be at the DFCS office on time. I arrived back at the Fairburn Road DFCS office and was directed to the waiting room. The waiting room was full but not to capacity, which was a relief. There were plenty of empty chairs, and already seated were the faces of people who had stood in the rain with me earlier that morning. Also seated was the woman with the alcohol who was still lit and jolly and still reeking of pure grain alcohol. Next to her was the one-tooth friend chomping on Bugles. There were mothers like me who now had their children with them who were a lot younger than my son, so the waiting room sounded like a daycare with the crying children. The room was not the cleanest, and it took me a minute to find two seats that didn't look like someone had had a bowel movement accident on them. On the wall were two large signs. One said, "YOU HAVE A CHOICE. GET A JOB." I found this sign to be very offensive because all I want to do was get a job, and believe me, if it wasn't for a jacked-up background thanks to our legal system, I would be working instead of standing in the rain and sitting in a crying waiting room for help. The other sign said something about "STOP WELFARE. WORK." It was the second sign that triggered childhood memories of my mother and her talk of welfare and beating the system to care for six children and an alcoholic spouse. Then it hit me. I was sitting in the welfare department, something I swore to myself I would never do because of what it put my mother through. Everyone was calling it DFCS, but this was welfare. I sat there totally disgusted with myself and thought, *God, what have I to do with welfare? I'm your daughter, and I do not belong here.* However, somewhere deep within me I felt, I was going through this mess for someone else, and I was confident that the Lord was going to bring me out of it all , but the big question was *when?* I don't know where they got the name "welfare" because no one in the waiting room was faring well. However, I was angry that some of the sisters had their nails and weaves done, and practically everyone there had a better cell phone than I did. In fact, someone even had a BlackBerry. How could they afford a BlackBerry on welfare?!? Here I was, having worked all my life, and the first time I needed help, I was unable to get it. Due to my inability to get employment, I had to give up getting my monthly manicure and pedicure (which was a treat to me). My hair hadn't been colored or permed in months, so I had to resort to wearing wigs. In fact, my roots were so thick the wig rose up on my head, so I had to assure it was secured with hair pins on my head. One day, I scared the dickens out of my son. I had washed my hair and cornrowed it, showing my then totally head of gray. When my son came home from school, the first thing he yelled was, "Momma, what happened to your hair?" I was so embarrassed; I must have looked like Moses to him (to quote my sister). I cancelled my Blockbuster membership (my son and I really missed having the DVDs mailed to us), the cable had been turned off, and my cell phone was a $19 Tracfone where I had to buy a card to get "units" for a call. At the end of the day, "wisdom is the principal thing," according to Proverbs

I sat there and explained to my son, to the best of my ability, what welfare was. I also explained the importance for him to be obedient to his teachers and learn from them, so he could graduate, go to college, or become an entrepreneur never having to depend on welfare for anything. Lastly, I assured him of God's ability to deliver us from all our challenges. I was glad to see he had a lot of homework, which I had him do while we were waiting. However, he too was becoming a challenge, wanting me to do his homework for him instead of figuring out the answers for himself. Between my son bugging me, the crying babies, and the loud talking of the woman in her state of inebriety, all I could do to maintain sanity was to plug in my iPod and tune out the world until I heard number sixty called.

Two and a half hours later, I heard my number called and, thanking Jesus, I went to the back room with my son to complete the paperwork. The staff member I was assigned to was less than friendly. In fact, she acted as if she really did not want to be bothered by anyone. She never smiled, and when I greeted her, she never responded. I ignored this and continued to smile because I needed this unhappy person to complete my papers correctly. Fifteen minutes later, the staff member had completed my paperwork. I sat there with my mouth open as I couldn't believe that I went through an entire day for a fifteen-minute process of completing paperwork. She pushed the papers toward me and said, "Sign this." Ironically, she became very irritated because I sat there reading the information before signing it. She started breathing hard through her nose and rolling her eyes. When I asked her a question about the expectations going forward, she barked that I had to meet eligibility. When I asked when I would find this out, she never answered me, so I had to repeat the question twice before she barked, "You're eligible." I had to pull information out of her regarding follow up. I learned that after my all-day drama with DFCS and welfare, plus the hours of standing in the rain, I still had to wait six to eight weeks for the check to come in the mail and wait two weeks for a pink slip. She never told me what the pink slip was for, but I learned later that this is like an approved voucher for the forthcoming money. In addition to this, it would be six to eight weeks before I would receive the money to pay for the utilities, and during that time I had to maintain my utilities. I was told that if the utilities were shut off before the money came, that money would go back to the organization, and it would not be used to get the utilities back on! Can you imagine that? I said to the woman, "I hope you never have to go through this." Her response was to say she had been there, done that. I responded with surprise, stating that I would think that someone having gone through welfare drama would be a little more compassionate. At that, she seemed to soften and stated that she just tries to be cool to avoid being stressed out. She further stated the negatives of being stressed out. I totally agreed with her and wished her a blessed holiday and got the heck out of Dodge. I wanted to say to her that an attitude adjustment would help to lower her stress also. She claimed that she was being the way she was to avoid stress; however, her every action indicated that she was already stressed out!

Oh well, my day was done with DFCS, and I couldn't exit the building fast enough. I never looked back, heading straight to my car with my son and thoughts of what I was going to fix him for dinner. I ended my day in prayer, thanking God for helping me endure the rain, for helping me to patiently wait at various times throughout the day, thanking Him for number sixty, and for helping me achieve the goal for assistance. I thanked Him for helping me realize how blessed I was, despite my circumstance, and for the revelation knowledge of what my mother went through raising us on welfare, and He helped me to see the impact of the welfare system on our society. Lastly, I thanked God for my bed and a pillow to lay my head down on as I fell fast asleep, exhausted from the day's events.

It was three weeks before Christmas, and I was determined that my son would have a great Christmas, despite my lack of employment. I called the governor's office, the state office of adoptions, my post-adoption caseworker, his school principal, and anyone I could think of for assistance in meeting the desires on his Christmas list. I think the final straw for me was when my son was sitting in the backseat of our car while I was driving home from church. He had written a Christmas list, along with some other children I was carpooling to the rehearsal for the church's Christmas production that morning. However, it was just the two of us driving home from church. He held up his list and said, "Mommy, here is my Christmas list, but I wrote it for July which is my birthday. Hopefully by then, you'll have a job." I thought how thoughtful it was for my baby to think that way, and I said, "Son, we both know God, and He will provide what you need and what you want. Just make sure you're praying for what you want." My heart ached at this small comment from my son, and deep inside, I knew that he really wanted his wish list to be granted on Christmas day, just like any other child. I could see the concern in his eyes as he thought about the possibility of not having any gifts, let alone a tree, for Christmas.

Isaiah had to receive allergy shots, which the doctor felt was triggering his asthma. Therefore, twice a week we were sitting in the immunologist's office for over an hour, so he could get his shots, two in each arm. It seemed a bit much for such a young boy of eight, but it did help because his breathing treatments at night were needed less often. After he got his shots, we had to wait in the office for thirty minutes in case of a reaction. It was during one of those waiting periods that I pulled over ten gray hairs from my son's scalp. He kept egging me on to find more and pull them. I felt guilty as I sat there pulling his gray, wondering if I was the cause of his gray hairs. Unfortunately, when I worry, he worries, and no matter how hard I try to hide my concern, my son knows me as well as I know him. Concealing the day-to-day drama of negotiating with debtors and creditors is not an easy task. I had to keep reminding myself about the faithfulness of God, no matter how long it seemed. I wanted to be with family in New York or New Jersey, but the funds were not available. I wanted to see multiple gifts under the tree for my son, but the funds were not available. I wanted a tree in our home, but the funds were not available, but God is faithful.

It was three weeks before Christmas, but by the end of week one, we had a Christmas tree, thanks to a dear friend who had placed some money in a Thanksgiving Day card, which I had failed to open until then. Thank God for prompting me to open and read the card before discarding it. I felt if someone took the time to send me a card, the least I could do was take the time to read it. I'm glad I did, and my son and I happily drove to several stores looking for the cheapest but freshest Christmas tree. We'd had an artificial tree for several years, and I really wanted a fresh tree that year. I also needed to get into the Christmas spirit for the sake of my son and not allow depression to sneak in as most people do around the holidays. I was already missing my auntie, who was also my godmother, and her yearly Christmas card. She went to be with the Lord that September, and that was our first Christmas without a card from her or a call to her from me to say Merry Christmas. My son had selected the perfect tree, which was under twenty dollars and still very full and fresh. We played Christmas music in the car and sang along all the way home with the tree on top of the car. Since we had a huge cat, I let the tree just sit in the stand in the house overnight, so he could get used to it. The next day, we decorated it, and boy was it a beautiful tree, despite its emptiness. My son mentioned the fact that we had no gifts to put under it, and I reminded him of God's faithfulness.

Two weeks before Christmas, I received a call from a volunteer who gave me names of two places to go for help, on a Saturday and the following Saturday. The first place was at a hotel where she claimed I would be able to "shop for household items." She did not know the name of the place and was barely able to give me an address. The second place was Toys for Tots, but again, she was unable to give any kind of directions how to get there. She was able to tell me what was near the facility, so I was able to pull up MapQuest. The first place was thirty-four miles from where I lived, but I thought if I was able to shop for household items, it may be well worth the trip. However, when I got to the place, it was just a small hotel room with two tables loaded with rags from what looked like a thrift shop or someone's basement. Most of the clothes were wrinkled and smelly; none of the clothing was for an eight-year-old child, but rather was for adults.

All the clothing needed ironing except for a few adult sizes T-shirts that were still in the plastic covering. There were some infant toys still in their package but not many. Yet there were at least fifteen people going through these clothes as if they were the last to be found on the planet. There were even some Ingles shopping bags which I hoped were donated by Ingles for the people to put their rags in. I was so disappointed that I had to laugh at the incident. I remember calling my sister and telling her that I'd just driven thirty-four miles for a bag of rags. Sometimes you have to laugh at a matter to keep from crying (which is what I really felt like doing). I had just finished rehearsing for the Christmas production at my church where I was the overseer for the performing arts ministry. After dealing with over twenty children, plus adults, and being up since six o'clock in the morning, all I wanted to do was go home and chill. However, when you have a need, you can't afford to be choosy, and I certainly did not want to miss out on what could be a blessing. Nevertheless, my sister and I had a good laugh, and I drove home hoping that the next place would be far better the following Saturday.

The following Saturday, I drove to downtown Atlanta for the Toys for Tots to a building that looked like a gym. At first, there was so much confusion and disorganization that I wasn't sure if I was even at the right place. However, as I got closer to the door and stood in line to be serviced, I saw that they had a table set up with people checking off the names of those who were authorized to participate. I saw many people being turned away, probably people from the neighborhood who heard about the function. I remember praying, *Lord, I sure hope my name is on the list*. After a short wait, it was my turn, and, thank God, my name was on the list. The volunteer told me to be sure to bring my son because it was a party. There was no party whatsoever. However, it was well put together despite some confusion, and it started an hour late. There were encouraging words for those of us who were still unemployed during the holiday season, and there were offers of a church home for those who did not have one. There were tables set up for information regarding first-time home buyers, the Department of Labor, how to write a resume, and so on. They also had food in white Styrofoam coverings for a small lunch. In addition to this, there were black garbage bags with some toys in them for the children which had the names on the bags, and lastly was a heavy box for each family. I had received six toys for my son, one which was appropriate for a toddler, which was not a waste because we knew just who to bless with this toy. In the box was all sorts of canned goods and a bag of white potatoes. The potatoes were mostly spoiled, but there were about four good ones. The canned goods were great, like cut green beans, pork and beans, corn beef hash, a small canned ham, and all kinds of soups. I was so grateful for what I had received and thankful to God. I prayed for God to bless each and every person who had a part in this blessing. I even had the opportunity to meet the volunteer whom I had spoken with on the phone. She was so much more professional in person than when I had spoken with her on the phone. I was grateful for the favor of God shown to my son, who was excited about the black bag,. I at least had some toys to put under the tree. They even had a brother who gladly carried the heavy box to my car, and I remember thinking that I hope these people didn't think that I was perpetrating as someone in need, since I still had my Mercedes, mint condition car. I didn't have time to get a lunch box for my son, and shamefully, I felt too embarrassed to go back and ask for one after I had received the bag of toys and the box. I was rushing to get to the church for the dress rehearsal for the Christmas production, and after telling everyone else not to be late, I definitely could not be late. My son was in rare form in the back seat, and I was glad to see this. For the whole week, once the tree was up, he had a saddened face because he saw no toys under the tree. Little did he know that I had long been speaking with different people at DFCS demanding help.

The week before Christmas, I received a call from a Mrs. Craw, from another organization, who said that they had adopted my family for Christmas. She said that she got my name from DFCS and wanted to know my son's Christmas list, which I gladly provided to her. Much to my surprise, she also asked me what *I* wanted for Christmas, which took me a minute to answer. I had been so busy thinking about my son that I never thought about what I wanted; it took me some time to answer. Not wanting to hold her up, I requested some Yankee Candles, something nice to wear to church, a coat, or anything from Bath and Body Works. I provided her with my address, and she informed me that she would be delivering the items to my home on the Tuesday before Christmas. To that I was so surprised, since I had become used to having to go to a certain place to pick up items or foods. I thanked her profusely, and we hung up. On the Tuesday morning before Christmas, Mrs. Craw and two other employees showed up to my home with a huge box. My son had *over fifty Christmas gifts*, all beautifully wrapped. Ms. Craw and her coworkers gently placed each gift under the Christmas tree while I stood there like a fool covered with tears of joy. I had not expected such an act of kindness. They had my son open a few of his gifts, so they could take pictures to bring to their coworkers and boss. I was even blessed with a skirt, a dress and jacket set, and candles. They weren't Yankee, but they were scented, and who cares when you have nothing. I've learned to be content in whatever situation I found myself in, and right then I was so grateful. The Word says give and it shall be given to you in good measure, pressed down, and shaken together shall *men* (which also means women) give unto your bosom. I was thankful that over the years I'd been a cheerful giver, and I was convinced that the Christmas blessing was a result of my past seed sowing. We took pictures, and I got out my camcorder, and I had my son speak to their boss on the phone to thank him for the wonderful gifts. Please be advised that those were no cheap gifts. My son had asked for a

PlayStation 2, which he got with five different games, and he wanted a lightsaber from Star Wars which I knew was $15 at Walmart, and he got both. He also requested new sneakers for school and shoes for church, and he got both (His sneakers were NIKE, something I don't even buy him!), not to mention numerous toys and clothes that had not been on his list. I was also blessed with a gift certificate for $15 for Kroger's and a $10 gift certificate for Red Lobster (one of my favorite places). My son and I were blessed with both gifts and food. I was glad for my years of donating both money and canned goods to the poor and homeless. Little did I know that I would be one in need of some of the services I had helped to supply in the past. God truly showed up for us!

My son and I received more that Christmas of my unemployment than all the years I'd been employed, put together! Not to say that it was the life because anyone with common sense would tell you that it's far better to have your own and not have to depend on others. Remember, I had to work to get help. It didn't come by osmosis. I made numerous calls and visits and sent letters and emails, and then I made some more calls. I stood in the rain, stood in lines, and sat in waiting rooms *for hours!* I was put on hold, disconnected, fussed at, and cussed at, but I continued to pursue help to assure our Christmas was just as good as if I had still been working. I had never asked for any help in the past, but I was asking then on behalf of my son and demanding that I get what I felt we deserved. After seeing people in the welfare office with BlackBerry's, I wasn't about to be denied help in my time of need, not from God or man. It was time consuming, frustrating, aggravating, and humbling. I felt beat down, exhausted, humiliated, and embarrassed. However, in the end, my son and I had a blessed Christmas, no thanks to our legal system. I didn't have to wrap one gift, nor did I have to shop for one gift. I had the means to get the food I wanted for Christmas. And that year, even I was blessed with gifts under the tree (something that only occurred when I could afford to go home to my sister's). I give all praises to God who is a God of abundance!

CHAPTER 7. THE VICTORY

**"But thanks be to God, which giveth us the victory
through our Lord Jesus Christ."
1 Corinthians 15:57 KJV**

In 2009, I finally had my day in court to face allegations of cruelty to children or child abuse. I went to court with total peace, knowing that I already had the victory. At that point, for the law to prosecute me based on false allegations and trumped up pictures (one which showed my son grinning from ear to ear, flexing his muscles), would be to state that it was perfectly fine for my son to live with this "abusive" parent for the past three years without supervision and or intervention from outside resources like DFCS, who had long ago closed the case. Meanwhile, the courts were trying to figure out what or when would be a good time to go to trial. All praises be to God for a different judge being appointed to my case, who was totally shocked that the case had been dragged out for so long while my career went dwindling down the tube. He was totally in sync with me concerning my ability to care for my son and I, as well as the importance of having a clean record for future employment should I decide to continue in my current profession. As for my attorney who had abandoned me due to lack of payment, among other things, he was not present at my hearing. However, I told the judge that I no longer had any legal representation and had tried for the past three months prior to court to obtain a public defender, all without success. I also told him that I waived any rights to legal representation, and I was totally prepared to represent myself to assure that my case was tried that day without further delay. The ADA present was yet another new one, which meant a total of *ten* ADAs who had had my case in their hands, and none of them came to court prepared to go to trial because their murder cases and other cases were more important since I hadn't been jailed. The current ADA stated that he had had my case for several weeks but claimed no progress due to an inability to reach my attorney who had failed to return any of his calls. Of course, he did not know at the time that I no longer had an attorney, and my former attorney was not courteous enough to return the call to advise the ADA that he was no longer representing me. However, the judge assured me that he would hear my case that day. I was shocked to see my attorney two hours later, storming into the courtroom, visibly upset at having been summoned to court on my behalf by the judge. As soon as the judge made a ruling on a previous case, my former attorney jumped up in front of everyone else, stating apologies to the court, *but* he was no longer representing me. The judge waved him off and demanded him to give a summary of what had been going on with my case. I thanked God that despite his refusal to represent me—and he was very short tempered with me—my attorney still had enough Jesus within to represent me well. After all my praying, I was convinced that neither my attorney nor anyone else could mistreat me, even if they wanted to. God, my ultimate judge, was on my side, and no weapon formed against me could ever prosper or succeed. My attorney very eloquently provided a short, but detailed, synopsis of my case which mimicked what I had told the judge earlier. The bottom line was the fact that my son was still living in my household without supervision and had been so for the past three years. I came to court with an abundance of evidence, which included my son's current behaviors, suspensions, and expulsions since the 2006 accusation. In less than ten minutes, my case was over, "deadlocked," and the judge assured me that the felony charge would be removed from my record. He further stated that he would send me confirmation of his decision in the mail and asked for me to leave my address with him. The judge did, in fact, send me his decision in the mail; however, little did I know that the clearing of my record was far from being over. Just as I thought the saga had ended, another one began, and it would be another, entirely different, battle to get my record expunged, so I could work. In the meantime, during all this waiting for trial, the country had gone into a recession, and many people had lost their jobs, including me. Therefore, even after having my record expunged, I realized it would still be another battle to obtain employment.

My trial was finally over, my days of taking time off were done, and burning up gas and spending my money on parking for court were finally over. The stronghold, the black cloud over my head, had finally dissipated. However, I still felt like a chained animal who, after having had the chain for so long, still stayed within the boundaries once the chains were removed, not realizing that it was truly free; or think of the theory of the insects in a jar who fought so hard for freedom, constantly hitting the lid of the jar until exhaustion took over. However, once the lid was removed, they never once tried to escape, even though their freedom was at hand. I had suffered verbal abuse and slander at the hands of CPS and members of the law, been persecuted by church members and so-called friends, experienced an attempted prosecution by the numerous ADAs, had my character defamed, lost income, lost employment, become unable to do the simple things in life like take my son to a matinee or treat myself to a manicure, been reduced to wearing wigs because I couldn't afford a perm, and the list went on for three whole years. Looking back, I can only thank God for His continued strength and comfort during this time. During the end of the third year, I finally told my family what had happened and was glad to receive their support, especially from my sister to whom I was close, but I had feared sharing my dilemma with her because I knew that at times she could be very judgmental. However, she had witnessed firsthand my son's catabolic fits of rage and anger. However, at the time, with her being so far away while I was going through my hell, I hadn't really thought to call her, for there was nothing she could do. There had been nothing anyone could do for my son and I, except (and I had initially forgotten this) *pray*. My body had become immune to high stress levels, and I had the full head of gray to prove it. However, because of my relationship with Jesus Christ, I was able to maintain my sanity. I think anyone else going through this without the help of the Lord would have ended up in a mental institution or worse. I knew I must pick up the pieces and continue with the legalities to assure that my record was expunged, which would be another whole time-consuming process. My flesh wanted to take the teacher who called DFCS, despite her knowledge of my son's off-the-chain and unusual behavior, and have her punished for her crimes concerning my son and me. She made our lives a living hell for more than three whole years. I recently saw her in the school hall, and she could hardly look at me. I was so tempted to say something, anything, to her, but what? I feared that whatever I would have to say would not come out holy or Christian. I knew I would need to find it in my heart to forgive her for that, and I prayed for God's help.

I could sense the tension and relief in my son who was then eight years old and was ecstatic to learn that all the court appearances were finally over. Although I never brought him to court, he knew when and had an idea of why I was going to court because I always had to find someone to keep him for me or pick him up from school for me. His behavior seemed to change a little for the better since my last court appearance, and I was sure he' was not feeling my stress any longer. My poor baby. How many times had I had to assure him that all was well (even when I felt all hell was breaking loose)? There were times he felt he was to blame and said he felt guilty which broke my heart. I had many talks with my son, assuring him that what I was going through was no fault of his, assuring him of my unconditional love and that we would get through it together. At times, I felt like such a failure because I could not shield my son from the hurt, the stares, the rejection, the gossip, the pain, and the anger of a world which was about to end, a world losing hope, a world not seeking Jesus, a world without love. From ages five to eight, my son also went through a hell of his own, not knowing from day to day if he would still have his mommy, the only person who truly loved him. Several times he would ask me, "Mommy, you'll never leave me, right?" and while I assured him I would not, in my heart I hoped my affirmation would be fulfilled. My son reminded me that I had promised not to leave him before, but he was taken from school, and although this was not my fault, he was too young to understand this, so all I could do was apologize profusely to him and hold him tightly.

It was finally time for healing for the both of us—healing in our spirits, souls, and bodies—and we trusted in our Lord to complete this process expeditiously. For me, since adopting my son, it had been healing from years of hearing negativity from people who assumed to know me, people who would see me weekly and had even served with me, yet did not really know me, or else they would have kept their unkind words to themselves. I still hear ringing in my ears—accusations from two groups of people. One group was stating I was being too harsh or mean with my son, while the other group was accusing me of spoiling him and being too lenient. But what do people really know about rearing children when they compared my son with their own children, not realizing that each child was created unique, notwithstanding the factor of adoption versus biological birth. The best teacher is God Himself, who is the greatest parent of all. However, as easy as it is to say forget people and not be in bondage to them, the reality is that it still hurts when cruel and untrue things are spoken due to their lack of knowledge. There have been a small number of people who, after witnessing my son in action for an hour or so, came back to apologize for their misunderstanding of why I do what I do. It's hard to come back from defamation of character, and I'd already decided that people were going to believe what they wanted, regardless, and I just needed to make sure my life was reflective of God in me. If God was pleased with me, then it really didn't matter what others thought, especially since they did not care for my son and me. Still, the pain came and went, but with each day, it was getting better. It had been three years of being beat down and broken. However, I believed in God for a quick recovery of everything lost emotionally, spiritually, financially, and physically.

CHAPTER 8. THE SAGA CONTINUES

"For our light affliction, which is but for a moment, worketh for us a far more exceeding and eternal weight of glory; while we look not at the things which are seen, but at the things which are not seen; for the things which are seen are temporal; but the things which are not seen are eternal."
2 Corinthians 4:17-18 KJV

Along with the emotional and financial healing was also the healing of my record which needed to be expunged. Although the paperwork took the arresting institution and me less than two minutes to complete, the DA's office was less than accommodating to help finalize the process. No one in the DA's office could give me a consistent answer or advice on the process for getting my record expunged, and I kept getting the runaround, even after driving to the DA's office and speaking with staff face-to-face. By the time I got the correct information, I had completed a self-guided tour of the superior court building. After getting the correct information and completing all I needed to do, the documents were turned in. The expunging of my record was still pending due to the incompetence of the legal system. There was no regard for the urgency of clearing my record, so I could return to work to support my son, whom I had allegedly abused. I was told that the district attorney was too busy and important to return my calls or answer my letters. All my calls to him via his secretary had been unreturned, the emails unanswered, and the certified letters, although signed for, received no response, yet taxpayer money is what pays the DA's salary. It would take another book just to explain all the red tape and mazes I'd gone through to get my record cleared, so I could resume work and care for my son and me. However, no one at the DA's office gave a hoot, and it was apparent that clearing my record was going to take much longer than I had anticipated, so my next move was to look for an entrepreneurship to earn a living. Perhaps this was God's plan for me all along, so I wouldn't have to depend on people to allow me time off for my son's appointments, or get permission to leave work to go to his school for a meeting, or even get permission to take time off for a vacation. However, to make any money, you need money to get started. I regretted having to exhaust my funds in order to make ends meet after losing my job during a recession, but living is a priority, and I had no options. God bless America!

It took another *four months* to get the Georgia Criminal Investigating Center (GCIC) to clear my record. This was mostly due to paperwork getting lost in the sauce and the right hand not knowing what the left hand was doing. I had to stay on top of the staff and those in authority at least every two weeks to follow up on my record information. My urgency and need to work was not important or as urgent to them. While they told me they understood, they clearly really didn't, and most of the time, the staff used the excuse of being understaffed as the reason for their incompetence in losing my documents in the first place. In April 2009, I was finally able to go to the local police department and have my record pulled, which was cleared. However, when I called the third-party company who had me dismissed from the one job I had landed in October 2008, due to felony charges, I was told that my record had not been cleared on their end. I then had to submit my documentation from the GCIC to this third-party company, so they could conduct their own investigation.

You would think that they could pull my record from the GCIC for themselves. I had to follow up as this particular company was frequently used for background checks by many healthcare companies and institutions. To add insult to injury, I learned that my record was still open for public viewing through the superior court. Being a licensed professional in the medical profession, employers would often check for court documents as well as the background checks. To close my records at the court would require the judge's authorization to the court clerk. This was most frustrating for me. Just when I thought I could now find a job and care for my son and me, another obstacle came in to play. I thought perhaps the Lord was trying to tell me to release my nursing career forever, but I still submitted applications. It would be another long, drawn-out battle to have my records expunged and sealed from the court and prevent it from being available for public viewing.

That being said, no one at the DA's office, the law library, or the record department could tell me the procedure in Fulton County for having one's record sealed or removed from public viewing at the court. One told me to complete a petition and wait for another court date to, once again, appear before the judge. However, this did not make sense because the judge had already given his authority to have my record cleared, so I could return to work during what would have been my trial or, should I say, the dismissal of my trial. In fact, per the case manager for the judge, he was willing to sign whatever I needed to have signed to clear me for work but not even he knew exactly what needed to be signed or approved. Then I was told at the law library to draft a letter mimicking the petition but word it to reflect a request to have my records sealed from the court documents. That also was not the right procedure but then no one exactly knew what the right procedure was! The case manager for the judge was getting upset with me because I did not have the answers, yet he worked daily with the judge and the legal system! Lastly, I went back to the DA's office and while waiting for his staff to try to find the answer to my simple question of how to get my record sealed from public viewing, in walked the DA himself! I felt like I had finally seen the President of the United States. I grabbed him and told him how long I had been trying to just touch base with him and why. Surprisingly, he was very cordial and promised to help me clear my record, but I'd dealt with broken promises before from our legal system. He assured me it would be handled and then told his staff to have Ms. So-and-So handle my case and left. However, he no sooner left when Ms. So-and-So had me waiting for another twenty minutes, just to tell me that they didn't handle such requests, and she referred me back to my original place of request. She did promise (another promise) to follow up with the chief in charge of the expungement department and promised to contact me.

By the time it was June, I was still trying to clear my record, so I could work. I had since started a business working from home, but like any business, it takes time to grow and mature before any finances are seen. One Saturday morning, I woke up early, got my son and myself dressed, and headed to a nearby church to stand in yet another line for a box of food. Despite the early time of the morning, the sun was high and hot, and the line was already long. The United States was dealing with a recession, the people were dealing with depression, and I was dealing with my relationship with God. As I stood in that line, I remember thanking God that at least that time it wasn't raining outside, and though the sun was hot, I'd rather feel the warmth of the sun than the freezing rain I had felt standing in a different line not long ago. I wondered if I was in the right place or position in life to receive the fullness of the Lord. I thought of things I may have said or done to deserve being in that position. I had reruns of sermons playing in my head with some pastors saying that if all hell was breaking lose around you, then we were to look at what we were doing wrong; yet another group of pastors said that it meant we were doing something right, and the Devil was mad, trying to deceive us. I'd rather the latter in my thinking, and as I looked around at the people in that line, I thought, *I am truly blessed*. There were people in line on crutches, in wheelchairs, missing limbs, suffering with impaired vision and other physical disabilities, yet here they were in line waiting for a box of canned goods. I was no better than they were, but by the grace of God, I was able to stand in that line on my own two feet. I could see, I could hear, and I had the use of all my limbs. I had a sound body and a sound mind; I was blessed. I struck up a conversation with the ladies standing in line with me, and my son was already playing with the children of the mothers standing before and behind me.

I looked across the lawn at my son who was clueless of the magnitude of my financial situation. He was still living the status quo, expecting to be bought something each time we were near a store. He never received the information that I was no longer working and did not have the cash I use to have. To him, nothing had changed because to him, he was still eating, still had clothes on his back, still had our house, and I was still driving the Mercedes. To my son, Mom was still wealthy. As I thought about how my son perceived the situation, it didn't sound like such a bad idea to just join him and stop trying to always correct him. *One of the marks of a good mother is when your child doesn't realize just how poor you really are, despite all the physical and emotional struggles!*

Demonic Forces Against Children's Spirits, or DFCS as they call it, is a vast system that destroys our future, and they profit while doing so. If nothing else, DFCS taught my son how to be manipulative at a very young age. I remember seeing social workers teaching foster children how to smile and be polite prior to the quarterly social gathering where parents wanting to adopt children would meet with foster children in downtown Atlanta in a designated area. It reminded me of being in a pet store, looking through the window at the cages of puppies. The one selected would always be the one who was the friendliest and friskiest. Likewise, the children were taught to smile and be polite and not be afraid to ask the adults to be their mommies or daddies. I witnessed social workers taking the children aside and asking them, Don't you want a home and a mommy and daddy? Well, you better smile." The children have more sense than the social workers. After all, what do the children have to smile about? They've been separated from their biological parents for whatever reason, shuffled from foster home to foster home, some separated from siblings, some have been abused, and here they are on display in the hopes of being "purchased" by a family. It's modern-day *slavery* at its best, but the children are still told to *smile*. This is not *Candid Camera*. This is no joke. This is reality.

From the experience of being taken from school and placed back in foster care for just a few weeks, my son was taught (by DFCS not the foster parents), that "no adult can touch him." He was returned to me very fragile yet very smart-mouthed and more rebellious toward authority. He would tell his teachers, "Leave me alone, or I'm going to punch you in your groin," and would carry out his threat because he didn't feel like reading or doing his math. He was angrier than I'd ever seen him and had a self-defeated attitude. He was more of a bully which was his way of protecting himself from the world. Thank Jesus that my son has come a long, long way. However, we still have a ways to go. Since hearing that the court ordeals were finally over, I've seen a calmness about him that wasn't there before. He continues to tell me daily that he loves me while kissing me all over, something he has always done but has increased. I've no doubt my son loves me, and he knows I love him. However, his healing is spiritual and emotional, knowing that his mother, like God, will never leave him and loves him unconditionally. He needs total deliverance from separation anxiety and the spirit of rejection. He also needs to learn about respect for self and for authority. Although his healing began years ago, due to the trauma of DFCS at birth, and again in 2006, we were starting all over again in 2009 beginning with the basics. God, however, has always been and will always be able to deliver him. I just have to be patient and remind myself that a delay from the Lord does not mean denial. It's a process, and like any process, it takes time. How long? Only our God knows. However, I must forever stand on His Word for all victories, knowing that both my son and I are in the forefront of God's memory. I must keep reminding myself that this too shall pass. It's a light affliction, and if I can see it, then it's subject to change. I could see my lack. I could see my setback. I could see my dwindled bank account. I could see my gas tank on empty. I could see the picture of a gas pump on my dashboard telling me it was time to get more gas. I could see the empty king size bed where only I (and occasionally my son) slept due to being a single mom. I could see the struggles with bill collectors when they were not paid. I could see the electricity or cable being shut off due to nonpayment. I could see myself standing in a food line for food or a bill line for money. I could see my son's face when he couldn't understand why we couldn't go on our Florida vacation. I could see that in spite of clearing my record, I was still being denied a job because HR rarely gets rid of a bad background check on you once they have the response. Instead, they file it with your resume for future reference. *And since I could see all those things and more, they were subject to change, said the Lord!*

CHAPTER 9. A MOTHER'S LOVE

"Sing, O barren woman, you who never bore a child; burst in to song, shout for joy, you who were never in labor; because more are the children of the desolate woman than of her who has a husband, says the Lord."
Isaiah 54:1 KJV

I once heard a woman say that a mother's love can only be understood by a mother because of the nine months spent carrying the child in the womb; however, I totally disagree. *Anyone can have a baby if they are physically fit, but not everyone can be a mother.* I have seen many mothers go through nine months of carrying a child, go through labor and childbirth, yet still lack the skills required to care for another little human. Being a mother requires a special anointing that only God can deliver. To be a true and bona fide mother requires a relationship with God the Father and an understanding of His Word in action. I don't know how the parents of today can even begin to raise children without the Holy Spirit's consultation and direction. There is no mother on this planet that can convince me that I don't love my son just as much as they love their biological offspring. Without hesitation, I would risk my life to save my son, as would any mother. I'm my son's biggest fan, closest friend (after Jesus), protector, provider, comforter (second to the Holy Spirit), and confidante.

Adoption is the most selfless act of love; it's the heart's ability to raise someone else's child as your own. It is to love, nurture, and raise up that child in the way that he or she should be and do it according to God's law. Despite all the hell I've gone through and all the challenges surrounding my adoption, my love for my son has never wavered or changed. A mother's love is compared to the love of God, a love that never changes and a love that is unconditional. For me, my love doubles for this child who is not just my adopted son, but my only son and my only child. I often thought of adopting a sibling for my son, but after going through so much in such a short period of time, I doubt if my spirit, soul, and body could handle another explosive experience. However, if the Lord has led you to adopt one of His children out of the system, He will give you the stamina, grace, and guidance to endure until the end.

It takes a mother to dry teary eyes, cleanse and kiss a boo-boo before applying a bandage, wipe a face full of spaghetti sauce before cleaning the high chair and floor, wipe a bottom full of poop before eating her own meal, wake up in the middle of the night to give a breathing treatment, or calm a child after a nightmare, assuring him or her of continued security, and still maintain your regular job while pursuing an education and continuing to smile and serve the child, spouse (if applicable), and public. A mother's love is one that never gives up, despite all the agony or trouble a child puts a parent through. There is always, in the back of the mind, that ray of hope that your child will one day do great things. Despite half the world telling you about statistics, mannerisms, and behaviors of your child, you cling to the hope and God-given revelation that your child will not fall prey to society. A mother knows her child better than the child knows himself or herself because she has spent time with her child, and no teacher, relative, or friend can know her child better than she does. Her love for her child surpasses all understanding, not because she has carried the child in her womb for eight or nine months, but because she is a *mother*.

It would take another book to write about the sacrifices a mother makes for the sake of her children. Oftentimes, it's at the expense of a disgruntled spouse or family member. For those of you who are anointed mothers, you can relate to the numerous sacrifices we make for our children, not because of fear of DFCS, a spouse, or the public, but because of our undying love for our children. A coworker of mine once shared with me that she keeps a picture of her son on her desk in front of her to remind her daily why she works at a job she despises. This was her encouragement or motivation for staying at her place of employment. Many times, parents (and this goes for fathers also), must do like David did in the Bible and encourage ourselves in the Lord). There may not be anyone around to give us a good word, and it is at these times that we must encourage our own selves like David did in the Lord. I'm well aware that there are also some single fathers out there, but this chapter is dedicated to those of us who are single mothers since I'm able to speak from firsthand experience as a single mother. Although single parents at times play a dual role of mother and father, a mother can never truly be a father to her child, and a father can never truly be a mother. A single father will sacrifice a football game to attend his daughter's dance recital, and a mother will sacrifice her manicure or pedicure to take her son to basketball practice or karate; that's what parents do. We sacrifice for our children, and it doesn't matter if you're a biological parent or an adoptive parent. However, I've had some biological parents tell me that they're not sure they could have or would have done what I did for my son. They couldn't say for sure if they would have gone to jail for their child; it's one of those things that you can't really predict—how you would respond in a certain situation or given circumstance. Suppose your child was grown and knew better than to break the law; would you put your life on the line and tell a lie in court to keep him or her out of jail? I like to think that as parents, we would make our decision based on the best interest of our child. Yet, a mother's love transcends all understanding.

Like a marriage, when you decide to adopt, you're committed to that child for life whether for richer or poorer, in sickness and in health, in good times and bad, and, at times, forsaking your own family. I've had to, at times, help my son deal with rejection while being rejected by my own family because of my son's behaviors. Though I know my family loves me, there are times when all the cousins would get together or one of my sisters may have invited my other sisters over for a holiday with the kids, but my son and I would not get the invite because no one really felt like dealing with my son's behaviors. They have never said this to me directly; it's always indirectly, an unspoken decision they made based on my son's *past* behaviors. Of course, at times there is always the excuse that, "I don't mind dealing with him (my son), but it's my husband," as a reason for the rejection, which I do understand, but it doesn't stop the hurt and the pain. I've pretty much accepted the fact that my son will not grow up as close to his cousins as I would have loved since he has no siblings to play with at home. I can't deny the hurt I've felt because of this, especially since I was raised in a fairly large family, and we were all pretty close, so naturally I would want this for my son as well. Of course, having to deal with rejection on a personal basis has made me almost an expert at doing all I can to assure that my son doesn't feel rejected, say in school or at a class party or wherever he goes; he's been hurt enough. In hindsight, I must admit that perhaps because I am single and did not have a spouse to confide in, many times I would call my sisters, all who have children of their own except one, and I would vent my anger or frustrations at a particular thing my son did or did not do. I regret this now, since it certainly did not help build a relationship with my son and his aunts. It is for this reason also that I feel it is best to be married and adopt as opposed to being single because you will definitely need that special person to vent to or just get some insight or another opinion.

Family cannot understand what my baby has gone through, which greatly differs from what their children have or have not gone through; sometimes they don't understand there is no comparison, and the "kids will be kids" cliché doesn't apply. It's hard to relate to first being rejected by your biological parents (both mother and father), rejected by the families of those parents, rejected by numerous foster parents, and rejected by numerous daycares and schools. I've felt the pain in my heart many times at seeing my son's eyes when hearing an adult tell me not to bring him back to school, or being made fun of by classmates who don't understand, and the list goes on. Yet my son, when he was old enough to understand a little more, would say to me, "Mommy, I want to be good, but there's something inside of me that's angry." I understand.

Through all the hurt and pain I've felt, hurt by the mouths of those who just don't know or understand and pained by my helpless situation that I could do nothing about, I had to cling to the fact that God was and still is in control. I'm still not sure why I've had to endure this hardship, other than to know of a surety that it's not for me but for someone else. Perhaps there is a parent out there who has a son or daughter like mine and needed to hear my story to know that they are not alone, and there is someone else who's gone through something similar; or maybe my story is for the nonbeliever who thinks that man is always in control of their own lives and destinies. Perhaps, my story is for the one who is also considering adoption as an option. My recommendation is to never give up, cave in, or quit. Cling to your hope and your faith which only needs to be the size of a mustard seed. Love like you've never loved before, yet fight like you've never fought before. This is what I had to do in order to win this battle, keeping in mind that the battle is the Lord's and not mine to fight in the first place. My love for my son kept me strong, kept me fighting, kept me believing, and kept me hoping. Now I understand better why it is written that, "Love conquers all."

CHAPTER 10. REFLECTIONS

"For I reckon that the sufferings of this present time are not worthy to be compared with the glory which shall be revealed in us."
Romans 8:18 KJV

I've been asked many times if I regret adopting a child, and my answer is always, without wavering, an absolute and profound NO! Despite the persecutions I endured, such as people judging me incorrectly, the lies, the accusations, and the drama that comes with rearing any child or children, my son has also brought me unspeakable joy. This is the kind of joy that only a God-given child can bring and is the result of my adoption of him, after all the mess has settled, and it's the end of a day. My son is not the cause of all the hell I've been through, but rather a dysfunctional legal system, a teacher, and a social worker who was a busybody. My joy is in knowing that I'm doing the will of God who set this adoption up in the first place. I've no regrets in knowing that I've saved an innocent child from the talons of a demon called DFCS which promotes recycling children in and out of foster homes and juvenile courts. I've no regrets in knowing that there is a foster parent out there who will not profit from my son being in their home. Now please don't misunderstand me; there are some great foster parents out there. However, there are also those who take advantage of the system and harbor a herd of foster children in their usually large home to collect their stipend (which isn't much until you add all the children's stipends together). They'll take the children's money, buy food to cook, say, a pot of beans to feed them all, using half or less of the money collected from one child, and then pocket the rest of the money for themselves. Meanwhile, the children will wear hand-me-downs or clothing purchased for a dollar in a thrift store, while these foster parents walk around with new weaves, manicures, pedicures, and designer clothing. I know what I'm talking about because I've seen them firsthand and spoken with them; in fact, I met them initially right at DFCS during my MAPP training. Believe me; they do exist! Sadly, I'm sure DFCS is aware of their existence, but they are so desperate to find even a temporary placement for the children that they turn a blind eye from this wickedness. So no, I have no regrets adopting my son, and yes, I would do it again. However, I would probably not use DFCS and would go with a private adoption providing I could afford it. The only reason I would go private is to cut out all the red tape drama and bureaucracy associated with adoptions through the Department of Family and Children Services.

Having said all that, I must confess that if I had been made aware of my son's challenges before my adoption of him, there are some things I would have done differently. For example, some of my parenting skills would have been different. I should have kept my son home once he bruised himself on the bedpost, but I felt I had nothing to hide, and the bruise was so small it surely wouldn't be a big deal, but boy was I wrong. Some of the people I employed for assistance would have been different, and regardless of a special needs scholarship which has a requirement that the child be in the public school system for a year, I would have never removed my son from a private education to pursue this scholarship. I would have kept him in a private school at least until his completion of elementary school in order to have a more solid foundation of morals and values. I was amazed at my son's ability to pick up slang language, swagger, and behaviorisms, just from being in the public school for one week! Of course, children will pick up mannerisms and behaviors in any school, but it varies to the degree that I feel is more prevalent in the public school system where there is a lack of disciplining the children for fear of DFCS, CPS, or disgruntled parents.

Children did not ask to be born and are not responsible for the way adults handle our worldly affairs. According to "AdoptUsKids" website, Sept. 9, 2013 "Georgia had approximately 14,000 children in foster care last year". According to Kids Count Data Center, Apr.13, 2020 "Nationwide in 2018, 52% of youth in foster care system were males and 48% were females, according to Child Trends, which analyzed data from the Adoption and Foster Care Analysis and Reporting System." Kidscount.org. Lastly, according to DFCS, as of August 2021, Georgia has approximately 11,921 children in foster care: Asian-27, Black-5729, White-6060, Native Am./Alaska-10, Native Hawaiian/ other Pacific-6, Other-89. Demographics of Children in Foster Care website. I'm not sure I agree with the accuracy of this count as there has been far more children in foster care over the years and the number had not appeared to declined that much. Adoptions have not been on an all time high and there has always been a push to adopt. According to DFCS, it is much easier to find placement for African American females than it is for African American males because of a stereotype that implies that girls are easier to raise up and nurture than boys. That being said, it also appears that there are more African American males in foster care than females. Being the mother of a male child, I find that males are just as challenging as females, for boys have their issues as future men and girls as future women. The bottom line is that cliché "children will be children", and regardless of gender, they both require love, care, and a lot of work.

Although the law requires that foster children attend school, rarely are they educated in the perils of life. They leave a system feeling helpless, hopeless, and homeless. They often are clueless about their biological parents or family roots and are left feeling alone and abandoned. Many suffer from depression and lack of self-esteem. Though I've been told of programs to prepare these children for a life outside the system, these programs are few and far between. So, you tell me what the benefits of foster homes are, other than to make a profit for the government and temporarily keep some children off the street.

According to "Welfare Watch," an article written in October 2008, foster homes are typically larger homes, have a larger number of children, have a larger ratio of children to adults, and the foster parents are less likely to be married couple households and are more likely to be single parent or households with cohabiting couples. With respect to socioeconomic measures, analysis shows that households with foster children, when compared to all households with children, are more likely to have severe financial housing burdens (more than thirty percent of income on housing), more likely to be low income families (income less than twenty percent of poverty line), they receive public assistance with the care, are most likely to have a householder or spouse who did not complete high school or college and did not work the previous year, or less likely to have a householder or spouse who worked full time in the previous year. With these statistics, it's no wonder that foster children age out of the system with fifty-one percent being unemployed, thirty percent ending up on public assistance, and twenty-five percent ending up homeless. We won't even mention morals or values because as a rule, they don't exist!

We spend billions on bureaucracy and bull, and we pay billions of dollars to bail out companies facing bankruptcy due to their flagrant spending habits, yet we can't afford to improve care for our children who didn't ask to come here in the first place. What about the children? It's bad enough that the superpower United States fails to take care of its elderly; the least we can do is care for our future. We hear talks and slogans like "No child left behind," yet that is exactly what we are doing, leaving our children behind. I still see teenagers graduating who can't read the back of a milk carton. They walk around with pants below their butts or skirts barely below the butts, belly buttons in full view of the public, and they think it is "fly" or "dope" (if this word isn't outdated yet). My son, at age eight, could tell me about the latest names for clothing styles, the latest video games, all about Xboxes, PSPs, and Game Boys, but I have to fight with him to read a book, do his math, or go to school. There's even a law in the state of Georgia which allows a teacher to exercise his or her right not to teach a child, which I think is an outrage! If you have a problem son or a child with ADHD or any behavior issues (like my son), and they are a challenge in a teacher's class, that teacher can have your child transferred to another teacher's class *without your permission or notification!* I know what I'm talking about because my son's kindergarten teacher (in the public school) decided in February 2006 to exercise her right not to continue to teach my son, and I was not notified, nor did they have the courtesy to let my son know that morning when he arrived to school that he was being transferred. He told me he thought he was being punished for something he had done the day before when he was told to go to another teacher's room for the day. He had no idea that this was to be his new teacher for the remainder of the year. I remember seeing how hurt his face was when the principal (assuming I had been notified), explained this law to us. I could sense my son's feeling of once again being rejected. I was hurt beyond measure as I was this teacher's "classroom parent," responsible for all the class parties and assistance with field trips, and I was a darn good one! Of course, the last party for the school year was the Valentine's Day party, and I always made sure that my son's class had the best parties. This teacher was so treacherous as to wait until after the last party of the school year before she made her decision. To add insult to injury, as close as I'd worked with her, she didn't even have the guts or decent courtesy to pull me aside and tell me of her decision, and to this day, I don't know the reason for her decision, but I do know that she could care less about my son, and her decision was totally selfish. Perhaps it was a blessing that he was no longer in her class as her actions were cold and spineless.

Despite all the drama associated with my case, I still strongly encourage adoption of our children out of the system. I think, however, that it's much easier for adoption to occur in a two-parent home rather than a single-parent home. Be ready to do a lot of research on your own concerning outside assistance post adoption. Unfortunately, at the time of the adoption of my son, I only received a raggedy suitcase, two Pampers, a short and shirt set, and a pair of oversize boots. I later learned that I was also supposed to have received an adoption packet which has information regarding post-adoption assistance. That packet was given to me in 2006 (five years later) during court proceedings, and by that time, my son had become too old to benefit from any of the assistance being offered. Be sure to read everything and then some as there is help available; however, if you don't know where to look or even that you need to look for something, you may miss out on a lot of valuable information. Sadly, during my dilemma, I was unable to get help from DFCS, CPS, and even the governor's office. Of course, people would respond to emails, but they dragged their feet responding to phone calls; however, the help they gave was to refer you to someone else who, when you called them, referred you to someone else. I call this "passing the buck," so you won't feel like they're not interested or not willing to help you. For the most part, I think that some folks want to help, but despite their titles and levels of positions, they really don't know where to refer you. I'm reminded of my frustration trying to get help with my utilities when everyone was referring me to the United

Way who would only give me a list of other numbers to call, most of which did not have any funds or required you to be a member of their church or religious affiliation in order to receive any assistance.

In regards to your son or daughter you plan on adopting, *please* make sure you carefully scrutinize the adoption organization, regardless of whether it's private or through DFCS, but especially if you're adopting through DFCS. I was given a folder (three days after my adoption) which had a lot of my son's family information in it—vital information; however, I didn't know to ask questions regarding my son's prior placements or how many homes he had been placed in during his stay in the system. I was so excited at having finally had a child placed with me that I didn't think of any possible issues until after the fact. I guess a part of me was afraid of what I might learn, but in the long run, if you don't have this information up front, it can come back later to take a chunk out of your life. Don't be afraid to read all the information and ask both the social worker and case-worker questions regarding the child. Ask to speak with the foster parents caring for the child. I was told that my son's foster parents were out of town (I later learned that this was a lie). The foster par-ents can be the key to knowing whether or not the child is a good fit for your family and vice versa. You can also consider being a foster parent first then adopting. This is called a foster/adopt parent. The benefits of adoption from being a foster parent first are that it allows you to learn the child and the child to learn you. It also helps deter-mine the fit in the family. The downside, however, is the possibility of the child being removed from you after there's been an emotional attachment or bonding within the family unit. I chose not to become a foster parent first. Due to a faulty legal system this backfired on me, and I was forced into fostering my son anyways before my adoption of him became final.

To avoid the emotional turmoil that comes with becoming attached to a child, I recommend that you first make sure there is a TPR (Termination of Parental Rights). That way, you won't have to worry years later, after you've been caring for this child and rearing him as your own, about long lost Uncle Joe or Granny Gable coming into your life to take your child from you. Make sure you get the TPR in writing! At the time of my adoption, I was told by the adoption caseworker and adoption social worker that there was a legal order for the TPR in place as DFCS knew in advance that I was only interested in children who had a TPR in place. However, two weeks after my adoption, I was told that the TPR had been overturned by the judge because the mother decided that she wanted her son back. I was outraged because by then, I had become attached to my son and vice versa. However, my only choice was either to give up my son and have him go back to the system or become a foster parent in the hopes that if the parent did not fulfill her obligations with the law, my son would permanently become mine. Of course I chose the latter, but with this decision came the hassles of arranging and complying with visits by the mother (who never showed up in spite of the numerous visits arranged), being available for visits by the CASA (Court Appointed Special Advocate) whose job was to assure the welfare of the child, have foster home evaluations, and be available for many court appearances where they determined the status of the mother's compliance to get off drugs, get a job, and find a place to live. The court mandates that the child should be present at those proceedings. That went on for a year before the judge admitted in court that he had made a mistake in overturning the TPR in the first place, and I was granted full adoption rights with a legal Termination of Parental Rights. However, I still went through a year of unnecessary hell; if only the paperwork had been correct in the first place. After all, I had done my homework!

Beware of hasty adoptions where DFCS just gives you a child without any paperwork! I was astonished by the way my initial contact for adoption was handled. I was called by DFCS, arrived at their office, met my son, and within thirty minutes and without any documentation, he was in my car and on the way to my home. I was so fearful of being stopped by the law and not having any proof that my child was given to me by DFCS. In hindsight, not only was it foolish of me to accept the child like that, but it was also illegal. For any lifetime commitment, there should be lengthy conversations and "getting to know you" time, just like a marriage. Request to spend some time alone with the child, even if it's just for thirty minutes, and I suggest taking at least thirty minutes to closely observe the child. If you can spend more time with him or her, all the better. If a child has behavior issues, such as ADHD, or is a hyperactive child, you will see this behavior manifest very quickly. Don't allow the system to pressure you into a quick adoption without exploring all the avenues concerning the child. A good adoption is one in which you have all the information, both good and bad, up front, so you can logically make a quality decision.

Pray! I chose to continue with my adoption because I know within my spirit that it was ordained by God. The circumstances leading up to my adoption were so unreal and orchestrated so well that only God could have planned it, and in case you didn't know, God is a master planner. It was only because of my prayers and the prayers of my family (both church and biological) that I am still standing and able to write this book instead of being in a mental institution. I thank God for the men of God that He placed in my life to teach me about learning the Word of God with simplicity and understanding or learning the word of faith or that God is my source. Each doctor or bishop or pastor has taught me so well the reality of God's Word being alive and having the ability to live and move and breath on the inside of me, which has impacted my life and those I have come into contact with. However, just reading God's Word and knowing about God's Word is not enough. *You must work the Word of God for yourself!* I thank God for godly mothers He placed in my life to assure me that I am a good mother, women who share their experiences with me regarding their children, and you know what, I've found it to be not so different than mine. I learned from them that children are children, regardless of being a biological or adopted, and mothers are not perfect. Likewise, I encourage you to seek Godly counsel and pray for answers, guidance, and perseverance. Don't just take the word of one person; rather, speak with many parents, especially parents who have adopted. Also, there is information that is available to you through your local DFCS office. Let them know that you would like to speak with parents of adoption, and make them help you with *all* unanswered questions.

Finally, know that despite a damaged Department of Family and Children Services and a defective legal system, which *do not work together* for the sake of the children, adoption is of God and is a god-like thing to do. You will be rewarded by God when you decide to do a selfless thing like adopt. To this day, I'm not certain why I was chosen to adopt my son, but I am sure that in God's timing, He will reveal all, as he did with my diamond in the rough called my son. I'm encouraged by famous people who were products of adoption, like Moses, Jamie Foxx, Babe Ruth, Bo Diddley, Dave Thomas (Wendy's), Malcolm X, Steve Jobs (founder of Apple and the iPod), Scott Hamilton, Marilyn Monroe, Dr. Ruth, Faith Hill, Melissa Gilbert, James Earl Jones, former-President Barack Obama, and even our Lord, Jesus Christ. Be encouraged, and know that when you decide to do something for God, he will provide you with the tools you will need to complete the task. "And I am convinced and sure of this very thing, that He who began a good work in you will continue until the day of Jesus Christ (right up to the time of His return), developing (that good work) and perfecting and bringing it to full completion in you" (Philippians 1:6 AMP).

BOOK II.

ADOLESCENT YEARS

CHAPTER 11. THE REBELLION

"For Rebellion is as the sin of witchcraft."
1 Samuel 15:23

Breathe...inhale, one, two, three, four, five; exhale, one, two, three, four, five... my life was on a roller coaster with a very innocent, abused adopted baby boy. I had to keep reminding myself to *breathe*. I don't know how many times I asked God if He was sure he wanted me as Isaiah's mom. I mean, I know God doesn't make mistakes, but could it be that just this once, He made an error? I'd been persecuted, jailed, defamed, ostracized, criticized, and, at times, abandoned by family, church, and friends! These were people who felt I never should have adopted a child in the first place. After all, I was a single woman. Who did I think I was to adopt a kid and have the nerve to adopt a male child, a *son* (as if I had a say in the sex of my child)! There were many nights I silently cried myself to sleep once my son was asleep. I never wanted to let him see me cry or unhappy, and I became so good at faking happiness in his presence which spilled over into faking happiness in public, *period*. I would smile in the choir stand singing hallelujah and dying inside, raising my hands and loving the Lord in corporate prayer and crying inside, all while trying to figure out why. I thought for sure I had heard God telling me to adopt this child, and the circumstances leading to his adoption were so uncanny and unusual. There was total peace in my spirit on the day of my son's adoption, and despite my son's initial behavior, it was a beautiful day, a gorgeous day, a blessed day. No, this was the will of God, no matter what it looked like.

Over the years during my struggles with juvenile court, my son continued to have struggles of his own. His temper tantrums were what I called catabolic fits of rage. When most children would eventually wear out and calm down, my son has been known to actively carry on for well over forty-five minutes; the longest tantrum he had was *two hours*. He would cry out loud, scream, bang his head on the floor or wall, wave his arms and hands all around, and at times bang them on the furniture. He would yell, "Ouch!" but keep hurting himself. Afterward, he would fall asleep on the floor; once, he didn't even wake up while I bathed him and put him to bed. I can't remember the bruising and pain I suffered in my attempts to protect him, for fear of further persecution from DFCS. There was a time he was so outrageous that I went inside my clothing closet to hide, cry, and pray while he carried on. I remember he stopped his tantrum and opened the closet door. I was so into my prayer that I didn't realize he had stopped his tantrum. He stood there in his innocence and said, "Mommy, I'm sorry I made you cry. I don't like 'falling out'" (which is what we called his tantrums). There was no particular trigger to his rage; however, I learned *years* later from his CASA (Court Appointed Special Advocate) that as an infant, he was abused by his biological mother's boyfriend and then later by subsequent foster parents. Thank God there was no sexual abuse! It's no wonder this baby was so full of rage, and God had designated *me* to bear with the rage of this child and bring out the love of Christ! It would take the Father, Son, *and* Holy Spirit to help me navigate through the journey. After all, I had no children of my own. Why, I wasn't even married, and many felt I was unworthy of being a single, adoptive parent. I had no experience with motherhood, but for years, God had had me in a position of working with children in my church, from the time I was a young adult in New York to the time I was an adult in Atlanta, Georgia. For years, I'd always found myself around children, and they would somehow gravitate toward me. Ironically, I never really liked pediatric nursing, neonatal nursing, or OB/GYN nursing. However, I was excellent in the rotations, being the only nurse in my group who was able to start an IV or give an injection to a child. In a moment—a blink of an eye—before the child realized it, he/she had been given the immunization. It was too quick for them to cry. I hated seeing children in pain. Last but certainly not least, I come from a family of five siblings (four girls and one boy). I was the oldest daughter, so there were six of us, and I had the responsibility of combing all my sisters' hair and getting them ready for school. I became an expert at corn-row braids. I was present for two of my sisters' births, and Momma taught me how to change diapers, care for the umbilicus (infant belly button), feed the baby, burp the baby, and bathe the baby, all except birth the baby. I guess in hindsight, the Lord was grooming me for motherhood; I just didn't know it.

My challenge was not having anyone to vent to. Sure, I prayed and spoke to God(notice I said I spoke to God and not with God; there is a difference); to speak with God means that you both communicate with each other. You speak then listen while He speaks and you listen; it's called prayer—a dialog; however, I didn't know any better and that which I did know was quickly forgotten once I was in the middle of a catabolic fit from my son. At times my prayer became a monologue instead of a dialog—just my constant complaining to God. I knew my son needed help that I could not render. However, every psychiatrist and psychologist I spoke with said he was too young, and no one would see me or my son until he was at least five years old. So, from two years to five years of age we struggled, and my son had already been through numerous daycares and preschool centers. He was dismissed from them all due to his behaviors. I was a working mom, and getting help from DFCS was like pulling teeth, though at age two, my adoption of my son was overturned due to court error; the one thing I did not want to do was the one thing I ended up having to do, and that was becoming a *foster parent*. I did not want my heart tied up with a child, only to have it ripped apart because parents changed their minds, or a family member came forth to claim the child. However, after DFCS offered me adoption, two weeks later, I received a call from DFCS telling me that Isaiah's mother had changed her mind, so the TPR (Termination of Parental Rights) was overturned. At that point, I had two choices: become a foster parent to give the biological parent a chance to get her act together or release the child back to DFCS custody. After seeing all this child had been through during the brief weeks that I had had him, God would not let me release him back to DFCS custody. There was no peace, so I agreed to foster care.

Foster care was a nightmare to me because I wanted to adopt! I didn't want to jump through hoops for the courts, cart my son back and forth to court to visit a mother who *never* showed up, and have unwanted visits to my home from the CASA and social workers to assure all was well. I didn't want to have to ask permission to go visit family out of town. All this was a waste of time as far as I was concerned. No one was listening to my pleas for help, and any advice given required me to jump through more hoops which ended up at a dead end... futile. I felt like a glorified babysitter for the Department of Family and Children Services. So, I continued to go from one daycare or preschool program to another and another because at the end of the day, I had to work. Of course, the state gave me a monthly stipend for Isaiah, but it wasn't even enough to feed him for a month, let alone provide clothing for him. We were kicked out of so many daycares and pre k programs that I lost count. We enrolled in Childcare Network, The Nest, Kids R Us, Kids World, ABC Kids, KinderCare, Early Learning Centers, Montessori schools, and private home schools—you name it. However, after two weeks to two months,

I was looking for yet another daycare center or pre k program. The so-called "Christian" daycares and programs sadly were less tolerant than the others. I could tell it was also taking its toll on my son whose main problem was change and a history of separation anxiety. His life had been disrupted so much that any kind of change would set him off into a fit of rage... can't say I blame him. It was hard for him to understand that his behavior was the reason for his numerous expulsions. I was at my wits' ends and out of solutions, but somehow, God would always direct me to yet another daycare or pre k program, and somehow, I managed to keep working. Ironically, I was also working on my doctorate at the time of my son's adoption, so I was still able to keep my grades up, studying in the wee hours while Isaiah slept. However, the older my son got, the harder the placement was. I stopped counting when we were expelled from school number *thirty-seven,* and he was only four years old!

Fear of going to jail again and losing my son kept me compulsive with keeping every bit of documentation from every daycare, pre k, and, later, elementary, middle, and high schools. It was because I kept such great records that my son is still with me. Had I not kept such accurate legal documentation on my son, I'm convinced that I would have lost him to the same system that had shoved him into my arms in the first place, and my life would have been behind bars for a bit,—a life ruined as a result of a record of "cruelty to children." I can't imagine a life without children when all of my life had revolved around children. Plus, I had a career which involved children! It's ironic that God never saw fit for me to marry and have my own biological child. I'll never understand this; after all, my body was physically capable of bearing and carrying a child of my own. I just never seemed to have met the right man to have a child with. I don't think I was being choosy or difficult or any of the many adjectives' men use to describe single women. There were many times in my life I cried and stressed over not being married and having children. However, I never came to the point of a compromise. I had many opportunities to compromise with a man. I just couldn't or rather wouldn't do it.

By the time my son was ready for elementary school, I had exhausted the list of schools in Georgia. I had exhausted my cash flow sending him to private schools, Christian schools, Montessori schools, and yes, even military school. At this point, I was a fully adoptive parent, as the state had finally realized that the biological mother had no intention of complying with the demands needed to get her son back. Therefore, I was on my own with little to no further help from the state. The stipend would no longer be provided, and I was literally *on my own!* I desperately wanted the best for my son, and I desperately wanted him to feel *wanted* and loved in his environment. In addition to all the school drama, his health was affected. His pediatrician had diagnosed him with asthma which, as a registered nurse, surprised me. I had never heard any wheezing or anything to indicate asthma; nevertheless, I'll never forget being in the pediatrician's office when she handed me her stethoscope to listen. My son's chest sounded like an accordion, and I learned that asthma does not always have an audible wheeze; sometimes the wheeze is silent except when heard through a stethoscope. I taught my son what to look for and feel for when his asthma acted up and told him to let Mommy know. He learns very fast, and thank God for it, because for the next six years, we would be using inhalers and nebulizer treatments. At age six, I learned my son had allergies to about everything you can imagine, except air. We were at the children's allergy clinic three times a week for him to receive two shots in each arm. My gut would wrench at each appointment seeing my baby subjected to yet another blow in life. If I could take the shots for him, I would, but I could not. Twelve shots a week equaled forty-eight shots a month which, over the course of time, would eventually dwindle down. He got used to the shots, but I never did. We were having to deal with both asthma treatments and allergy shots. To add insult to injury, the catabolic fits of anger continued and even worsened. I thought that my son would improve in elementary school due to peer pressure if nothing else; however, this only made him act up more; and as a result, he was even being bullied at school. After all, kids aren't used to seeing a classmate at that age "falling out" on the floor like a toddler. At about age six I found a great child psychologist. My son and I had been through several others, male and female, but my son didn't like them, and some would get impatient (believe it or not) with Isaiah and ended the session, while others would let him run all over the office with little to no conversation at all. One time, my son asked the psychologist such intelligent questions which I was also asking in my head. I had to laugh inside wondering who was the doctor and who was the patient. I felt like I was wasting time and gas driving all around metropolitan Atlanta to a psychologist who did *zip!* However, Dr. Williams (name changed) was the only one who really got through to my son. His behaviors were lessening, and anytime a child can later quote something he's learned from his doctor, you know something is working. There was finally impact! It was a good feeling! Dr. Williams was able to relate to Isaiah in a way no other doctor could. He would allow my son to "express himself," yet he maintained the discipline needed for my son to hear and grow. He also was linked to community programs for African American boys, many of which were either adopted or in a single-mother home. It was very interesting and educational for both Isaiah and me. When I asked my son why he liked this particular doctor so much, his answer was quick and simple, "He listens." There were programs on Saturdays where Isaiah would meet with boys his age from different areas in Atlanta to help develop his socialization skills. We would wake up early on those mornings. He would spend a whole day with the boys and counselors doing special things, all thanks to Dr. Williams. I also learned of a monthly gathering of families with adopted and foster children sponsored by an organization called Family Matters, and for the entire weekend, my son and I would do fun things. Sometimes we would stay at a hotel. These monthly one-weekend meetings were so special to me as there were all-day sessions I could attend to teach me various topics, given by top notch professionals, while my son would be elsewhere in the hotel having fun and playing games with other adopted or foster children his age. They would serve us *excellent* lunches (separate from our children), and in the evening, we all would meet and sit together as a family for an excellent dinner. It was a time of learning and relaxation for me. When Isaiah acted up, there were professionals around to deal with him; ironically, he rarely acted up at these events. He was around children, some who had the same challenges as him and some worse, and they all strangely understood each other. This was one good program indeed, and it was absolutely free except for travel. Families would meet from all over Georgia to support each other in dealing with their special needs children. The topics discussed were vital to us as foster and adoptive parents. Subjects ranged from various mental health issues to children with physical disabilities. Parents had an opportunity to share challenges they were going through, and the sessions became a real time for support. We would laugh together, and there were times we would actually cry together. We all loved children and wanted to be a means of support to them which is why we chose to become foster or adoptive parents. However, none of us had any idea what we would be facing with our new families. There wasn't any separation of races, creed, color, or ethnicity. We were parents of different races, colors, and nationalities; however, we all had the same concern—a child or children with issues—and we all needed help.

By the time he was thirteen years of age, he had built up enough immunity to no longer require allergy shots. We celebrated that entire weekend doing fun things. Unfortunately, with the coming of the teen years came the pushing of boundaries toward adulthood. My son was becoming more rebellious, saying to me almost daily,

"I'm a man" (something he learned during his short stay in DFCS custody). His teachers were complaining about his class disruptions and being an intentional distraction. He was pushing boundaries with me with talking back more and with other little things like preventing me from coming into his room by lightly shoving or attempting to prevent me from doing something he wanted or didn't want.

The saving grace in school was that I had fought tooth and nail for an IEP (Individualized Education Program). As stated in my previous chapter, per the principal at a public school, a teacher had the right to *not* teach your child; so, when my son acted up, the teacher would put him out of her room, and he went into another classroom. By law, they did not have to tell the parent of these changes; however, when you have a son with separation anxiety who is old enough to talk, he would come home every other day and tell me whose class he spent the day in. It got to the point that I didn't know who exactly my son's teacher was. We were not use to all this because before the exhaustion of my funds, my son went to private schools to avoid all the confusion and red tape associated with public schools. In private school, he would be with one teacher for homeroom, and though he may change to other teachers, he would be back with his homeroom teacher at the end of the day. My meeting with the teachers and principal at the public school was futile until I learned about an IEP via the internet.

This was a program which allowed a child to continue his learning within his designated class without being kicked out. It fostered socialization skills in that the student was allowed to remain with classroom peers. It assisted the teacher in that she could continue to teach her class with minimal disruptions as the child was assigned a special education teacher (usually not one of his regular teachers) who was with the child the entire day. It promoted discipline as the student was rewarded for good behavior. It helped to boost self-esteem as the student learned that he/she could be in his/her class the entire day without being kicked out and made fun of. It provided counseling services to both the parent and the student outside school hours, and the list goes on. Of course, this is my own personal opinion of the benefits of the IEP program. No one mentioned this IEP program to me. As I said, I did my own research on the internet. When you're a praying parent, the Holy Spirit guides you in a direction you're not even aware of, and I really stumbled upon the IEP information. You'd think with a program so great, the public school teachers would welcome it, especially if they have a challenging child in their class; however, I learned that some of the teachers at this school despised the day I learned about the IEP program, and to this day, I'm not exactly sure I know why. The IEP is only offered in public schools for kids in special education. Private schools can offer special education, but they are not required to, and the ones I went to did not offer it nor did they want to.

There are eight basic components of an Individualized Education Program. However, this may vary from school to school. I later learned some have six or seven components:

1. Current skill level

2. Annual goals

3. Special education services

4. Progress tracking

5. Duration of services

6. Testing adaptations

7. Transitional goals and services

8. Participation in mainstream classrooms

Of course, this meant that the teachers had to work with the IEP program, so eyes were on them as much as they were on the program itself. This is especially true when additional funds are going toward the school for this program. The IEP team members are:

- The parents

- At least one of the child's special education teachers or providers

- A representative of the school system

- At least one of the child's regular education teachers

It was not easy getting an IEP approval and the policies and procedures were... well, I can't think of the words at this time. Some of the rules I remembered for an IEP were for children with any of the following:

- Learning disabilities

- Attention deficit hyperactivity disorder (ADHD)

- Emotional disorders

- Cognitive disorders

- Autism

- Hearing impairment

- Visual impairment

- Speech or language impairment

The IEP must state the services and supports needed to reach the annual goals, and the school district is responsible for making sure the IEP is being followed as planned. I thank God I at least had support in this area once I was able to get approval. However, I was initially denied an IEP. You see, my son was extremely smart, and part of the problem was that he would complete the in-classroom work before his classmates and become bored while waiting for the rest of the class to finish. He would then become a distraction to the class. After numerous rounds of testing, he was negative for ALL the "Ds" (as I call it), ADHD (noted previously and there are seven of these), PDD (Pervasive Developmental Disorder), CD (Cognitive Disorder), and ODD (Oppositional Defiant Disorder). I was denied an IEP because my son had none of the listed disorders, physical disabilities, or learning disabilities that would qualify him for an IEP, though he clearly had a problem. I had planned to appeal the IEP decision, learned the due process, and did my own research. Based upon my findings and my son's signs and symptoms on the internet, I learned that my son exhibited, *hands down*, EBD (Emotional and Behavioral Disorder)! I sat there at the computer with my mouth hanging open like a drawbridge as I saw my son's behaviors displayed in words before my eyes. I was elated and full of praise as I thanked the Lord for finally finding the answer to all the drama. *God is good!* It had taken me a good week of daily research because I had a timeframe to appeal the denial, and I needed to be prepared if my case went to mediation. I presented my case myself, despite having representation in what is called a Dispute Resolution. This is a meeting with the Local Educational Agency (LEA) regarding the rights and services of a child with special needs. Since I had not been represented well in the past, I felt I could do a better job representing myself since I had done the research. My attorney was present, however, but it was more for moral support. At the end of my presentation of what my son truly had, which would fall under the category of emotional for qualification, I was granted the IEP. I came prepared with all the documentation from the internet of what EBD was, plus the documentation of my son's behaviors from his counselors, psychologists, and past teachers. I was shocked to see that *no one* at the resolution meeting knew what EBD was; in fact, they admitted that they had never heard of Emotional and Behavioral Disorder. At least I was granted an apology, and immediately, my son had an IEP in place to prevent him from being kicked out of his classes. He also got an assigned special education teacher. There was no need to go to mediation. Thank you, Jesus!

It's a lot of work and a pain in the ass, but I can't express the importance for parents to do their due diligence and fight for their children. Yours is the only voice they have in a world that's full of confusion and red tape bureaucracy. Instead of complaining about the school calling you at your job every minute regarding your child's behavior (like I initially did), get to the core of the problem and initiate a *solution*. Had I not taken the reins and spearheaded the research, my son would never have received his much-deserved and needed IEP, and he eventually would have become another statistic. I can't tell you how many times teachers wanted me to put him in a mental health type of school or a facility. Montessori schools (which I was frequently referred to) were not the answer because most of them were too slow for my son. While they promote children working at their own pace, they also had different "stations" the child could go to after completion of the station he or she was at. Since my son suffered from separation anxiety and hated frequent changes, going from station to station was not the answer. In fact, it frustrated him more. He would complete one station and head to the next while a child was still trying to complete a task at the same station. There would be two children at the same station, and a teacher would tell my son to go back to a station he had already completed, resulting in him having a meltdown. Of course, I tried it their way, only to hear that it wasn't a workable solution for him (something I already knew). At least I wasn't charged for the trial run of him attending these schools. I was amazed at how often I was advised that since African American males were more "difficult to manage and educate," they fare better at schools that *do not challenge their learning capacity!* What? *I would not allow my son to become a statistic... period!* I vowed to give my all to prevent that if that was at all possible. It was important for me to lay a good foundation for him.

Navigating the public school system was, at best, more like an obstacle course or maze. Even though I was a parent who worked with the teachers, many times I found the teachers to be very frustrating. Most of them were not equipped to handle special needs children, which I guess was one of the reasons why they did not support the IEP. This was understandable; however, there were very few who actually worked with my son and me. I truly thank God for the few that were on our side. I learned that there weren't many children who were in the IEP program at that particular school. I was glad to see that there was at least some consistency in the education of these children. I clung on to the hope that my fight for the IEP program was not in vain. I prayed for everyone involved in the program and that I would not experience the same drama as I did with DFCS.

CHAPTER 12. THE BATTLE

"For we wrestle not against flesh and blood, but against principalities, against powers, against the rulers of the darkness of this world, against spiritual wickedness in high places."
Ephesians 6:12 KJV

The year was 2006, and my son was pressing on through elementary school with his special education teacher. God sent an angel for my son's special education teacher. He was a Caucasian male, tall and skinny, with an appearance of a nerd. However, he was extremely patient and mild mannered. Many years later, my son confided in me how he knew he was taking advantage of this special education teacher and would intentionally do things that were disrespectful; however, he also said that he was his favorite teacher, and because of him, my son made many changes for the better. I never really got to thank him for the years of abuse he took from my son which somehow (in my spirit) I knew, long before my son's confession. I was surprised to hear Isaiah say that he wished he could have thanked his special education teacher for all the years he had put up with his abusive behavior. I was shocked to learn from my son some of the things he knowingly did to his special education teacher that were disrespectful. These were things that caused my eyes to bulge; however, his teacher never spoke a word to me about it. I was in constant communication with the man, and every time we spoke, he had words of encouragement and positivity. We had good days and bad days, unfortunately more bad ones than good ones.

Isaiah was being suspended from school at least once or twice a month due to his behavior, despite having a special education teacher. I had to admit that the suspensions were justified as my son had hit a child, and once he had hit a child so hard in the afterschool program, it was only God who saved the child from a concussion and kept his parents from suing. Over the years, I found that my people weren't always as forgiving as other races. It's a sad but true fact, and I guess it's related to all the years of abuse our ancestors had to put up with to the point that some feel they would not take any mess from anyone, regardless of race, creed, color, or ethnicity. However, I thank God for this family who did not press charges, and I assured them that my son would be disciplined. It was so hard for me when Isaiah was suspended as I was still going to the office to work. It meant finding a sitter for my son as he was not old enough to be home alone, and even if he was, I did not trust him. He had proven to me more than once that he could be very manipulative. Plus, suspension was not a mini-vacation; he was home due to inappropriate behaviors in school. Because Isaiah had an IEP in place, he wasn't suspended for talking out loud in class, being a distraction, or even being disrespectful to his teacher. It was usually due to hitting another student. He knew better than to hit, and I was beginning to think he was doing it on purpose, so he would be home. On the days he was home, I made sure it was not pleasant for him. He had no TV and no cell phone, and his teachers would send home the schoolwork for the days he would be out on suspension. Sometimes, it would be new work, so I would have to learn how to help him do it.

We progressed, slowly but surely. Isaiah was beginning to like his special education teacher who followed him to every class (or so he told me), and the negative reports were decreasing. My son was exposed to the mother-son school dance, which was so cute. I couldn't believe how timid my son was when it was time to have a dance with his mom. It was really precious, and the school had done a great job. I was also on the PTA committee. I felt with all the trouble my son caused the teachers, the least I could do was participate somehow. I often felt guilty regarding his behaviors, even though I was doing all I could to prevent them. They also had a father-son breakfast, and I remember how sad my son was not having a dad or representative with him. His uncle could not make the breakfast when I had approached him about it, so at the last minute, I asked a brother at my church who was more than happy to be there with my son. I did not tell Isaiah as I wanted it to be a surprise to him, and boy was it! He lit up like a Christmas tree at seeing my brother in Christ, whom Isaiah calls "Uncle." That was a good day.

There was also the class trip to Washington, D.C. President Obama was in office, and everyone was excited about going to the White House. I really wanted my son to experience this. However, the school had already warned me that they could not provide any special monitoring for my son. Parents of the children had volunteered to oversee a few kids in the hotel room, but with my son never having done anything like that and having behavioral issues, I couldn't trust him with strangers, and the school did not want him to become a liability, which I fully understood. The school had prematurely arranged for my son to be in school in another teacher's class while his class was on the field trip. This meant being in another teacher's class for a week without his usual classmates. I saw the disappointment on my son's face, and he said to me, "Don't worry, Mommy. I'm used to being left out" (or something to that effect). That was enough for me to hear. I immediately set out to somehow, someway, come up with the money for the both of us!

The new principal was much younger than the previous one who had failed to tell me of my son's removal from the school when he was in first grade. I hated that I had to return to this school after the drama with DFCS. However, as stated in my previous chapter, the IEP could only be provided in a public school, and I was out of funds for another private school. In any event, this new principal was *dope!* She and her assistant both worked with Isaiah and me. My son liked both of them and, to some degree, treated them better than his teachers. However, I remember one day when Isaiah was having a bad morning. To give him some space, he was sent to the principal's office to do his work. Since he had a somewhat good relationship with her, his special education teacher was not required to be present. Well, I got a call at work to come to the school. It took me over an hour to get there, but by the time I arrived at the principal's office, I saw Isaiah at a table coloring quietly (the only thing missing was the halo over his head), the principal was at her desk, and the office looked like a tornado had come through it. She told me, "This is all Isaiah's doing," as she looked around her office. She further told me that she would not have called me had he cleaned up his mess, but he had refused. All I did was look at him and said, "Get busy," and he got up and cleaned up the office. Even with this behavior, the principal did not suspend him, but rather praised him for cleaning up her office. She understood my hardship with finding a sitter when Isaiah had to be home.

Since I also had a good relationship with the principal, I discussed me going on the D.C. trip with my son, so he could attend. She advised me that I would have to get permission from the school superintendent to be a chaperone, and I was already in crunch time since all the chaperones had already been submitted. I had a little less than two days, so I immediately drove to the Fulton County office of the superintendent, filled out some paperwork, and provided the necessary proof and documentation and took a photo ID. Now I had to come up with the payment *in full!* To this day, I have no memory of how I came up with the money for our trip, which included the bus ride, hotel room, and tour. I rushed to the principal's office who was so happy I barely made the deadline, and she pushed all my information through. So, two days before departure, when she asked me if I would mind having two other boys with me and my son in the hotel room, I was more than happy to do it.

The 2011 trip to D.C. was phenomenal! We all had T-shirts of the same color advertising the school we represented. We saw all the highlights of D.C.—the White House (of course), the monument, the Lincoln Memorial, even the museum. I saw the dress our First Lady Michelle Obama wore at the inauguration. Most importantly, I never had to correct my son about anything during the *entire trip!* He was even very respectful and well-mannered in the hotel room with the other boys. He shared treats and souvenirs at the end of the day. I was so floored. I kept waiting for the other shoe to drop, but it never did. Once we were all back home, I made it a point to take my son aside and tell him how proud I was of him. I assured him that he could be obedient all the time, just like he was on the trip. He was still beaming and said he was so happy. All I could do was thank God for making that happen. I felt that was an overall change for the better... or was it?

Fast forward a few months, and my son was graduating from elementary school. The ceremony was especially precious, and much to my surprise, my son received several awards. He was always smart academically, when he applied himself. The challenge was getting him to apply himself. I thanked all the staff for working with us over the years and especially the principal and assistant principal who provided me with tips on junior high preparation (something I wasn't particularly looking forward to). Prior to graduation, the children even got yearbooks. I never received a yearbook until junior high. I was so surprised to see my picture in the yearbook (more than once) at some of the functions. At the end of the graduation ceremony before we all said our good-byes, my son broke down. He cried so hard I couldn't believe it. He said he couldn't believe he did it (even with many of the staff telling him he *could* do it). He also said that this was the best school he'd ever been to. I think this was because it was the only school that didn't kick him out. He hugged my neck tight and thanked me, and that was worth all the hell I had gone through over the years. It gave my son a sense of belonging and pride to be a part of something for so long without being cast out. I held back tears as I thought of all the battles I had fought to get him through to graduation. I was pleased to see children who were once enemies to my son become friends with him, and they included him in their conversations. The trip to the White House brought about a camaraderie.

I will never take all the credit for Isaiah's completion of elementary school. It was none other than the good Lord who kept me going and showed favor on behalf of my son and me. There were many, *many* days I cried and wanted to just give up, even after bombarding heaven with prayers. There were times I thought the Lord was just plain tired of hearing me complain about the DFCS system, the school system, Isaiah's behavior, the teachers, the homework, the suspensions, my job, etc. I thank God that I'm not God, or I would have *zapped* myself a long time ago. It was comforting knowing that God doesn't make mistakes, and He appointed me as Isaiah's mother for a reason. I may not understand the why of it; however, I trusted that God knew exactly what He was doing! I also got a true revelation of the saying, "It takes a village to raise a child." *Amen!*

CHAPTER 13. TOUGH LOVE

"For the Lord disciplines and corrects those whom He Loves, and He punishes every son whom he receives and welcomes [to His heart]."
Hebrews 12:6 AMP

My son had just started junior high. I wish I could say that things were better for us, but that was unfortunately not the case. The curriculum for junior high did not include an IEP for my son. I was told point blank that my son would just have to be on his best behavior or be suspended or even expelled.He was older and on medication as I had been given a referral from his psychologist (behavioral health) to a psychiatrist (mental health). Since he was five years old, I'd been to more doctors' visits than letters in the alphabet. At least four times a week, I was taking my son to either a pediatrician, psychologist, allergists, or a psychiatrist. He was only taking one medication which I was told would help his EBD, a medication that was especially needed since he was no longer on an IEP, and he no longer required the allergy shots.

As a healthcare professional, I was aware of cumulative dose effects of medications. However, after over a month, I became wary of whether the medication was helping my son. The methylpheni-date (Concerta) was making my son act like a zombie, and I immediately had this stopped. Then he was put on Vyvanse and Adderall, but I refused to try Ritalin. It had appeared that the Vyvanse was the only medication that was halfway working. Over several months, it was a battle getting my son to take any medications as he was very resistant to it. As he got older, I had to make him open his mouth and stick out his tongue after administering the pill every morning before school. Some mornings there was an argument about him having to take the medications, and some mornings he would take it without argument.

Throughout the months in junior high, my son continued to be very challenging. We continued to go to weekly therapy and continued his medication. Sometimes I thought they were working, and other times, I wasn't so sure. He still had his tantrums which had escalated into punching holes in the walls or damaging physical property. Since I lost my new home in 2010 due to losing my job which downsized, punching holes in a rental home was going to cost me. I attempted to explain this to him, and he would say to me at thirteen years old, "I'm a man." I had to take the time to explain the difference between being a male and a man. Punching holes in the wall certainly did not make one "a man." Someone had told him along the way that he was a man without fully explaining to him exactly what being a man meant. Incomplete information about manhood and puberty was causing confusion. Somehow, he got the convoluted idea that he could come home and tell Mommy what to do. For those of us who are old school, you know that this does not work in a household with a single African American mother. As long as you're living in my home, you'll abide by my rules; however, I am also aware of the necessary caution in not being too rigid or overbearing.

To allow my son some autonomy and freedom (per our conversation and my working with him), I agreed to him being a "latchkey kid." I had never heard of this; however, my son told me that many of his friends were "latchkey kids." It was the beginning of the school year in August, and per his request, we decided to try something different. He was of age, and since his bus stopped in front of our house and literally came fifteen to twenty minutes after I left for work, I committed to trusting him to be alone for those fifteen minutes and to get his behind on the bus. It would also drop him off after school about thirty to forty minutes before I would get home for work. He had a cell phone and was to commit to calling me when he was home. I had to leave home at a certain time to drive to the MARTA and catch the train to work, or I would end up driving an hour and a half due north to Dunwoody. My son was fourteen and wanted me to start trusting him, so I agreed. He talked a *great* game, and I bought it all!

It was a sunny day in mid-August, and the children had been in school for about two weeks. I had gone to work as usual, and so far, the "latchkey kid" situation was working out well. I told my son how proud I was of him. However, on that particular day, I was feeling uneasy at work. Before I had left for work, my son and I had had a disagreement over something so simple I couldn't even recall it. It was not an argument—there wasn't any yelling—I simply had said no to something my son wanted to do. In any event, feeling uneasy, I advised my manager that I needed to leave work as I had a situation at home (my manager and director were aware of my special needs son), so I was allowed to leave. I felt so strong in my spirit that something was not right. I thought I'd go home and check on things, and if all was well, I would return to work as it was still early morning, and I had only been in the office for about thirty minutes.

I arrived at my ranch home to find the front door slightly ajar. I didn't know if I should call the police or what. I looked around the neighborhood which was, as usual, quiet for that time of morning. With my heart beating through my chest, I entered my home, slowly opening the door wider, while looking around for something to defend myself with if it was needed. I was breathing rapidly, and my heart was racing as I slowly entered the living room… nothing. The kitchen was straight ahead, and I could see there was nothing unusual. To my right was the hallway leading to the bedrooms. The first room was my son's, and his door was closed. I slowly opened the door, not knowing what to expect, and to my horror, his room was in total disarray. All his clothes were pulled out of the drawers and thrown all over the room. His bed sheets and bedspread were pulled off the bed and onto the floor. His mattresses were pulled apart. I then went to my bedroom and found that my bedroom was even worse. All my dresser drawers were pulled out, my dresser was turned over, my clothes were thrown all over, my jewelry box was broken with all my jewelry thrown all over, the mattress was literally off my bed along with the sheets, and the bedspread and pillows were all over the floor. As my eyes filled with tears, I went to my office to find my computer and monitor gone! I stood in the doorway in shock with my heart pounding away and a large lump in my throat. I called the police.

While waiting for the police, somewhere in the back of my mind I couldn't believe it was a robbery or break in. Somehow, I felt this was the work of my son, but I didn't want to believe it! As I quieted my mind and asked the Lord for help, I heard the Holy Spirit say, "Look! Your new color printer is still on the desk." As I looked at the printer, it was a confirmation that this was indeed the work of my son. I thought, why would a robber take an old computer and monitor and leave a brand-new printer. I tried to figure out where my son could have taken my computer and monitor in such a short amount of time while causing such destruction. He only had had fifteen minutes! I looked all over the house while waiting for the police, but I could not find my computer and monitor. I decided to call the school and check on my son. When the principal came on the line, she told me how great my son was. He had arrived at school on time and seemed to be having a wonderful morning so far. She even said he was in good spirits. Normally, I was used to hearing negatives about him, especially in the mornings which seemed to be his most challenging time, no matter how early I got him to bed the night before. In any event, I was at least glad he was having a great day at school.

Finally, the police arrived about twenty minutes later. They asked questions, and I told them I believed I know who did it. When I told them I believed my son had done it, they did not really believe me. They took notes and were looking around for my computer and monitor, which didn't take them long at all to find. One of the officers nonchalantly walked over to the garbage can and lifted the hood. Looking inside, he said, "Ma'am, I could be wrong, but this looks like a computer in here." I went over to the garbage can and saw my computer and monitor inside one of my white garbage bags and ever so carefully placed in the garbage can which, thank God, was not full. Funny, I didn't think to check our garbage can. The officers were kind and very apologetic on behalf of my son. You see, my son had been pushing boundaries which had caused the police to visit my home quite a few times just to talk to him. I had made friends with some of the officers at Fairburn Police Department and knowing I was a single mom, they would attempt to encourage Isaiah by talking to him, and sometimes they would give him a vivid picture of jail.

After the police left my home, I took the remaining hours to survey the mess. I couldn't believe the amount of damage done in such a short period of time. As I looked over his room, I heard the Holy Spirit directing me to look along the inside bedrails where his mattress should have been. I was shocked to see *all* of my son's daily pills lined up along the railing. To this day, I have no idea how he was able to cheek his medications while lifting his tongue up, and still not swallow it. The pills were whole. I couldn't understand it, especially since I was the one placing the pills in his mouth. It then became clear why he had been on a roller coaster of behaviors with an increased frequency of tantrums.

I busied myself cleaning up my room as best I could. I had hidden the computer and monitor as I did not want my son to know that they had been found. I really wanted to see his reaction when he got home from school. The bus stopped in front of the house, and Isaiah got off the bus and ran into the house, surprised to see me home. I said nothing. He went into his room, and boy, the drama was worthy of an Academy Award! "Momma, oh my God! What happened?" His eyes bulged, and he went to my room, saying "Oh my God! What happened?" I said nothing. He ran to my office, all anxious and full of concern. He said, "Momma, where's your computer?" I finally said that I guessed whoever broke into the house stole it. I asked if he had locked the door that morning. "Yes ma'am. The door was locked when I left." He could see that I was extremely saddened. He then went out the door; the garbage can was outside the front of the house, just to the left side of the garage. I quietly went out the door behind him and stood on the porch watching his every move, but he didn't see me. I saw him lift the top to the garbage can, and his eyes widened as he became perplexed. I saw all of this! He finally turned toward me and jumped at seeing me standing on the porch watching the whole drama unfold. "Looking for something?" I asked. he could not say a word. I finally said that if he was looking for my computer and monitor he threw in the garbage, the police had already found it. His eyes widened more. I said, "Yes, I called the police." I couldn't believe that he was still trying to pretend he knew nothing about what had happened. I also deserved an Academy Award because surprisingly, I was cool, calm, and collected. I slowly turned to go back into the house and calmly told him to go clean his room. He started out yelling, "Momma, I didn't do this!" I held up my hand to stop him and again told him to go clean his room as I walked away from him.

The word of God speaks about never correcting your child in anger. Lord knows, I was angry; however, I was more hurt and disappointed. I decided that right then was not a good time to discuss or deal out any discipline. I needed to get into God's presence for answers. I wished I had a man in my life or spouse to discuss the situation with. However, there was no greater person to discuss it with than the Lord, the Creator of my son. I calmly went into the kitchen to prepare dinner. I had already advised my manager that I would not be returning to work. My son adamantly refused to clean up his room. I calmly and softly, in an almost inaudible voice, said he would not eat dinner until the room was cleaned, and I walked away. I knew he was shocked at the change in my behavior. I normally would have been loud and dramatic; however, I began to realize that the older he got, the less effect being loud and agitated would have on him. He took *three hours* before he decided to start cleaning his room. It took him another two hours to get it back in order. It was now past his bedtime, and I knew he was hungry. I had his plate already fixed and sitting on top of the stove. He told me he was done, I checked his room, and I told him his food was on the stove which he nuked and ate. I was too exhausted to do anything more, and I was still trying to get my own room in order.

I could see that my son was getting closer and closer to crossing the line. He would gently shove or push me when walking past me during many of our teenage disputes. I told him on many occasions, "I will go to hell and back for you, but if you ever put your hands on me, it's over." That was all I would say while looking him straight in the eye. He once told me that DFCS told him I could never give him up, that I *had* to take care of him no matter what. I told my son not to believe everything DFCS told him. I knew that somehow those thirty days away from me in April years ago when he was placed back in the system, though temporary, were enough to undo all the work on values, morals, and foundation I had instilled in him. He was different in a way I couldn't describe, and I needed a new strategy to handle his rebellion. He was a teenager with tainted ideas of what a man was and what he wanted to do. I looked to the hills from whence cometh my help (paraphrase).

Corporal punishment would never work on my son, especially as a teenager. What would work were things like taking his cell phone for a few weeks or preventing him from playing his video games, things that he enjoyed after school. I remember one day asking him for his cell phone as punishment for being disrespectful to one of his teachers. He told me that he lost it. However, much later that evening, the Holy Spirit told me exactly where my son had hidden his cell. He had previously punched a hole in the wall in his room during one of his tantrums. I walked into his room and placed my hand inside that hole in the wall, praying I didn't touch anything alive or dangerous. As my hand moved inside the wall, almost to my shoulder, I reached his cell phone. As I walked back into the living room, holding up the cell phone, my son couldn't believe I had found it. He asked how I knew, and when I told him it was the Lord, he appeared to be humbled. Ironically, taking away his cell phone, though temporary, was more of a pain in the butt for me than it was for him as it would be more challenging for me to keep tabs on him. However, I needed to hold him accountable for his actions in school with his teacher.

September 9, 2014, is a day I shall always remember as another turning point in my life. It was early evening, and I was preparing to help my son with his homework. It required him to write a report about songs he liked and what impact they had had on his life or why he liked the song. Since he had already written the report, I told him I would type it up for him (to expedite getting the assignment done). Just as I was about to start the report, a sister from church called to ask if she could come over and use my laptop for some work she needed done. I thought this was a very unusual request from her, but her computer was down, and I had no problem with her coming over as I had both a laptop and desk computer (which I was currently using).

She arrived at my home, and we both sat in my home office to work, her on the laptop and me at my desk using the computer. As I was typing, I came to a particular paragraph in the report where my son had written that he liked a particular song, even though he knew the words were derogatory. I thought, *Derogatory... hmm...*, so I called my son and asked him what he meant. His response was disrespectful and defensive, demanding I just type what he had written. *What?* I thought, so I asked him again what exactly were the words to that song. When he refused to tell me, I said, "No problem. I'll Google the lyrics." As I was about to search Google, my son started to bang on the computer keys in attempt to prevent me from looking up the music. I remember slapping his hand away and continuing my search. As I was looking up the song, out of nowhere I felt a punch from behind me to my right cheek, knocking me completely off my chair. As I fell to the floor, my son, who was now over 180 pounds, jumped on top of me and began punching me in my face and head. The blows were coming so fast I could hardly breathe. I heard my girlfriend yelling at him to stop, but he wasn't listening. I remember thinking, *I'm going to die at the hands of my son*. As I saw my own blood flying, I yelled, "Jesus, help me!" and immediately, the blows stopped. I don't know what happened, but later that evening, my girlfriend said, with bulging eyes, that Isaiah went flying across the room (airborne) and was slammed up against the wall. As I stood up, I remember seeing him up against the wall, looking totally demonic. He didn't look like my son at all. His face was red, swollen, and contorted with eyes red and blazing. He looked crazed. As I tried to gather myself, I didn't realize my nose was bleeding until my girlfriend told me. Of course, she had called the police who thankfully arrived very quickly. Isaiah, who had calmed down a bit, appeared to be transforming back to himself again and was shocked at what he had just done. He kept yelling, "Oh my God! Oh my God!" he ran into the kitchen and grabbed a butcher knife and threatened to kill himself. I, still being Mom concerned for him and still bleeding, walked into the kitchen and somehow grabbed the knife out of his hand and shoved him into a chair, all in one quick motion. I had had enough and was pissed, though I didn't know where that extra boost of strength came from. Later, in hindsight, my girlfriend reminded me how I had placed my own life back in danger by walking up to my son who was standing there holding a knife. At that point, I wasn't thinking. All I knew was that the Devil had invaded my home, and I was mad as hell!

Thank God that the police who arrived were officers who knew my son and had spoken with him in the past. They took him outside to calm him down. I, on the other hand, was on an emergency call to his psychiatrist who advised me he would immediately make arrangements to have him committed to the Behavior Health Hospital for Adolescents. He also strongly advised me that under no circumstance was I to allow my son to return home. He told me that if I allowed my son to come back home, I may not live through another one of his tantrums. He had diagnosed my son with bipolar disorder with narcissistic tendencies. The officers took pictures of my bloody nose and face and completed their paperwork, then drove my son to the hospital. I was to follow in order complete the required paperwork as my son was a minor. My sister from church prayed with me before leaving to go home to her own family.

Driving to the hospital alone in my car, I was numb. I don't even remember how I got to the hospital. My mind was in torment as I tried to figure out what the hell had just happened. I was embarrassed, hurt, disappointed, angry, and sad, such a mixture of emotions with mental, physical, and spiritual pain. I had a multitude of questions for

God and wasn't hearing any answers. However, one thing stood out among the mess of evil—Jesus had my back and had sent his angels to defend me. I couldn't forget the image of my son flat against the wall and the fact that he had gone airborne! That night, I learned that demons are real, and so are angels. As a nurse approached me to complete his paperwork, I remembered filling out the forms. However, my mind was in another world, on another planet. I somehow managed to complete all that was needed to admit him, and thankfully, the staff had already heard from his doctor and given instructions for admitting orders. One of the nurses, seeing my own face and nose swollen, asked me if I was okay and wanted me to me seen by a doctor, but I assured her I was okay and that I was also a nurse. My pain was more emotional than physical.

The drive home seemed like I was driving into another state, which was strangely soothing to me. I wasn't anxious to get back to the scene of the crime. However, I didn't want to drive with my brain in another realm. When I finally made it home, in my loneliness, the flood gates broke, and I cried for what felt like eternity. I was too embarrassed to call anyone, and I knew there was nothing to be said which could soothe my broken spirit. I was even too numb to talk to God, if that makes any sense; I had finally reached my wits' end, a dimension of pure brokenness. I had never felt so helpless or so hopeless in my entire life. I was a survivor of an abusive relationship during my college years (thinking I was in love), and even that could not compare to what I was currently feeling. It took me five years of abuse to learn the difference between love and lust, permissive and possessive behaviors, how to love myself first, and what was just plain craziness. I hoped to God that whatever the lesson was to be learned would not take five years! I couldn't believe that my son, my only son, would ever put a hand on me, and in my quietness, I heard, "But he wasn't your son at that time," and I fell into a deep sleep.

As the days progressed, matters didn't get any better with me. I couldn't stop crying, and I was glad to be in a position at work where I could take some time off. Lord knows I needed it. However, I could only take three days off. I wasn't eating or sleeping, and at times I was shaking at the thought of the drama. I walked around my home like a zombie. I'm not a smoker or drinker, so there was nothing to dull my senses. I was so broken, and even though I called out to God in my brokenness, I wasn't hearing anything, which seemed worse to me. Strangely, I felt His *presence*. However, I didn't hear a word from the Lord. He was silent and, in that silence, I somehow knew I needed help—mental help. I contacted the EAP (Employee Assistance Program) which I knew would help me find a psychiatrist, and all information was confidential, especially if you did your own research, which I did. I met a wonderful female therapist and completed every session paid for by my employer. I wasn't too proud or embarrassed to receive that help because for the first time in a long time, I was taking care of *me!* I was told it would take at least six months to get me back on track to feeling like myself again. However, I did it in four months. I had weekly sessions. Sometimes, there was no talking, just tears. Other times, I would bear my soul, feeling like the worst creation on the planet, and still other times I was just plain angry. My therapist allowed me to work through all my different phrases of emotional healing. However, she wasn't one who spoke as someone who was religious or Christian. It wasn't until I finally tapped into my spirit and dependence on the Holy Spirit that I really started to heal. I felt the need to have to pray more and spend more time in His Presence for total healing, for resolution, and for power. Once I stopped beating myself down and realized how much God loved me, how he had saved me (in more ways than one), and how He had created me because of His love for me, I was able to accept what had happened to me and continue to live. My first step was to commit to forgiveness! My brokenness drove me closer to the Lord, and in His Presence, my healing was supernatural.

In the meantime, my son was still in the hospital where he was also receiving counseling sessions for his behaviors. I was contacted by his psychiatrist who had had him admitted; he warned me that the hospital would be getting in touch with me to pick him up as they had kept him in the facility as long as they could. However, he adamantly warned me *not* to pick him up from the hospital. He further warned me that after my refusal, the facility would get in touch with DFCS, and they would be calling me, but he told me not to give in. He stated again that if I brought my son back home, I may not live though another one of his tantrums. He assured me that DFCS would take care of him, but if I brought him home, I would be on my own again. Since I was receiving counseling myself, I was in a much better state of mind to think clearly, and I felt so much stronger. I could feel myself coming back to me, and as I prayed about picking up my son from the hospital, I received my confirmation to follow the doctor's orders to the letter and I did. It's called tough love. Though it hurt me so much more than my son, I truly believed he would come out a better person because of it because God was orchestrating our lives. So, with my heart in my hand and a lump in my throat, I gave my son back to the system I had wanted to save him from, and that time, it was voluntary. I thought about how God must have felt having to give up His only son for us! I remember feeling like my heart was literally splitting in two, and I knew that I could no longer care for my son as he had become unruly, challenging, blatantly disobedient, and abusive to me. I knew if something drastic was not done, he was headed for jail or worse, death. My cries for assistance from various state and local institutions were futile, if received at all. I was tired of the abuse from the system and abuse from my son. I knew I had to regain control of my life and that currently, this was not the abundant life promised to me, so it was time to think about me if I was going to survive this planet called Earth and this existence called Life.

Like clockwork, the facility made their calls to me, just like I was told, and when I refused to pick up my son, DFCS started calling after a few days with threats of putting me in jail. As stressful as this was and somewhat scary, I stuck to the plan and the doctor's orders and did not give up, cave in, or quit. I bombarded the doctor's cell phone, calling with fear of being jailed. However, with every call, he was so reassuring that everything would work out well. He was so calming and understood that it was a scary time and a fearful situation. Sure enough, after a few days, DFCS went to the facility and picked up my son. They called me a few days later to ask if I would mind bringing him some clothes, so I packed up my son's clothing and met the caseworker at DFCS.

For twelve and a half years, I had struggled as a single parent raising my son as best I could according to God's word. I had hoped that the Lord would send my soulmate, and I would marry and have a father for my son, sadly, that was never to be. Sometimes I nailed being a mother, and sometimes I missed the mark. After all, motherhood doesn't come with a manual. My son was almost fifteen years of age, and for the previous two years, he'd been telling me he was a man; now he would learn what being a man was really about. He was back in the system where he would learn to fend for himself—no more Momma running to the rescue. Adoption doesn't come easy for the teenager, so I already knew that my son would be in the system until he aged out at eighteen to twenty-one years of age. Depending on his behavior, he may end up in a good home. However, he will most likely go from home to home and bounce all around until he ends up in a new program or ages out. All I can do now is pray for him and follow him at a distance.

He will learn that being a man is not beating a woman, especially your mother. He will learn of the sacrifices I made to keep a roof over his head, food in his mouth, and clothes on his back. He will learn what it's like not to have his own private bedroom or any privacy for that matter. He will learn some of the ways of the world. Hopefully most will be good; after all, he has been given a good Christian foundation, regardless of how he acts. Being a woman, I am very limited in teaching my son how to be a man, but he has been exposed to the brothers in my life who took him under their wings until my son wasn't listening anymore. He so wanted to be free to do whatever he wanted, despite having more liberty than I ever had at his age. Now he will learn just how much freedom he really had. I guess I'd have to admit that my son was somewhat spoiled. I always wanted the best for him and still do.

I too had a lot to learn and experience with my son who's no longer in my life. I remember that during one of my counseling sessions, I shared how having him placed back in the system was like a death to me. Although he was still alive, I mourned for him as if he wasn't. I had to realize and accept my losses:

Motherhood and being a parent

Parental responsibilities

My self-esteem

My son physically being with me

The thought and ability to care for him

The joy of being at his high school graduation

Communication with school staff, homework, etc.

Prom preparation and dating

Communications with teen ministry

College preparation from application to arrival

Before I even met him, my son had always suffered from separation anxiety, which I feel is a reason for his issues with anger management. Neither one of us wanted this. However, I felt so strongly in my spirit that this separation was the best for both of us. I felt like I was no longer being effective as his mother, and the only resolution was to let him go, and if he returns, then my parenting was effective. This was also the only way I could force the state to help me help Isaiah become all that God had created him to be. Of course, my son will not understand my decision. However, in time, he will not only understand why I did this, but that my decision was the right one.

The final tearing in my heart was when I had to appear in court to terminate my parental rights. I begged the court to allow me to still be a part of his life while in DFCS custody. However, I was advised that per the law, I would either have to bring Isaiah back home and continue on my own or depart from him with no involvement at all, which is the TPR (Termination of Parental Rights). I thought, *Wow… how ironic. It was a TPR I needed in order to adopt this child, and now it is a TPR that is needed to bring him back in to the same system.* What a jacked up and messed up world we live in (forgive me, Lord). The world would rather have a TPR than just work with me by taking care of Isaiah and still allowing me to be a part of his life. Who knows, perhaps things would work out for the better for both of us. I was so hurt and angry by the court's laws, but I stuck to my initial decision.

Sitting in court was the first time I had seen Isaiah since the day of the assault. He looked well, very well in fact. And no, I'm not speaking of his clothing and attire; I am speaking of his spirit. His attitude was one of indifference. I couldn't tell exactly how he was feeling but then; he could always hide his feelings well, something learned from being a child of the system. He sat partially laid back in his chair and never once looked over at me. He had a look of confidence or assurance, perhaps an air of arrogance, and he had an obvious smirk on his face which lasted throughout the proceedings.

The entire process was about forty-five minutes long, and I was advised that there was no need for me to have an attorney present unless I chose otherwise. The judge was a sweet African American woman who, after reviewing all the information, still could not understand why I was requesting a TPR after raising my son for so many years. I explained I didn't want a TPR, but that the only way to receive more help for him from the state was to agree to one. Further, she was not aware of the assault I had previously suffered (something I think was conveniently left out of the report). When I explained that the assault was the last straw for me, of course she immediately understood and granted the TPR. At that, I saw my son's whole demeanor and countenance change. He wasn't so smug anymore. His face was one of utter surprise. Years later, he told me that DFCS told him I had no choice but to bring him back home as a TPR would never be granted. He was actually expecting to come home with me, and from the looks of things, I didn't see any remorse in his previous behavior, nor did I ever get an apology!

After the judge made her final decision and dismissed court, I walked over to my son and gave him a hug, kissed him on the forehead, and told him "I love you, no matter what." He never hugged me back or looked at me; he didn't say a word. Of course, I was crushed, but I didn't want to make a scene, so I slowly turned and walked out of court, alone. My brain was once again frozen, numb. I cried all the way across the parking lot to my car. I can't remember what I was thinking or if I was thinking at all. I was glad to have a session scheduled with my counselor later that day, which was just God happening to make my appointment on the same day of my court appearance. I really needed the therapy which helped me see things from a different perspective and with objectivity. I came home from my session, and although I can't remember much afterward, I remember praying which sealed the session I had earlier. For the first time in a long time, I slept well, without even having eaten any dinner.

CHAPTER 14. REDEMPTION

Redemption: the action of saving or being saved from sin, error, or evil.

Definitions from Oxford Languages

"He sent redemption unto his people: he hath commanded his covenant for ever: holy and reverend is his name."
Psalms 111:9 KJV

The first two years after my son was returned to the system were hell for me, especially the first few months. Despite therapy sessions and prayer, there were still many days I cried and was depressed. Everywhere I went reminded me of something my son and I had seen or done together. Passing an old school, a park, the pizza place, or Subway brought back memories of when we were together. I actually raced home from work one day, thinking I had to pick Isaiah up for his doctor's appointment, only to realize he was no longer with me. It was hard for me to cook for one person. I would walk past his room daily, only to stop and imagine him there or pretend to talk to him and pray for him. I'd go to work with a smile, but inside I was devastated.

I stayed away from church for fear of questions regarding where my son was as we were always seen together. What could I say? I truly didn't believe anyone would understand; after all, many felt I should never have adopted in the first place because I was a single woman. There were some who hardly spoke to me but asked about how my son and I were doing in a way as if they were expecting me to fail as a parent. It took me awhile to break away from people bondage. It was only after a prophecy came forth from the pastor confirming that my decision to adopt was from God that some came around and started treating my son and I like members of the human race. People mean well, however they can sometimes be so judgmental. I wasn't ready for all the questioning and scrutiny.

To help myself adjust to being alone again, one of the things I learned in therapy was to reflect not on my losses, but on what I've gained. Although my gains had not yet outnumbered my losses, they did serve to give me some comfort. I realized that I had gained the following: peace in my home and car, freedom to go wherever without the need for a sitter, the choice to cook or not, and I even had more money to spare. In fact, since I was now spending less, I had enough money saved up to move. It was very hard living in the same home, and my therapist even suggested that I relocate, which I took as a confirmation. My lease was about to expire in two months anyways, so I hung in there until the end of my lease and moved.

I thank God for my previous landlord who was a quiet Spanish man. He was always kind to my son and I the two years we lived there. His home was a three-bedroom ranch with a nice private yard in a quiet neighborhood. He told me not to worry about the holes in the wall because since I had kept his house so neat and clean with a few improvements of my own, he could patch up the holes in no time. I hoped my new landlord would be as kind. My new home was closer to my church. I was so glad to be moving away from both good and bad memories of times spent with my son. My new rental home was a two-story, single-family home with three bedrooms. It also had a yard and a nice privacy fence. I loved the fenced in the yard as I could literally walk out in my yard in under clothes, and no one could see a thing (not that I did this). I just loved the privacy and quietness. I needed it.

For the next three years, I poured myself into becoming a better me. Since I lived closer to my church, I got back to volunteering more, I worked on improving my credit score which had taken a hit due to all the private schools and training in attempts to help my son, and I pursued my passion in arts and entertainment. I started taking vacations alone out of the country! In 2018, I was blessed and purchased a brand new four-bedroom home, a brand new Mercedes, and a white puppy poodle named Oscar. Since I was spending less money, I came out of debt and drastically improved my credit score. No, I didn't hit the lottery or work an extra job; it was the blessings of the Lord, and He added no sorrow with it.

I secretly kept tabs on my son from a distance for about six months after he went back in to DFCS custody. After that, my contact lost track of his whereabouts. I remember frequently watching "Wednesday Child" on the news where they would show children up for adoption. I somehow hoped to see my son's face. However, deep within, I knew this wasn't possible. Teenage children, especially African American boys, were rarely adopted. All I could do was to continue to pray for him and ask God to show me where he was and how he was doing. I still missed my son, but I was in such a better place with a confirmation of having made the right decision.

Ironically, it was 2018, the year that my son would have graduated from high school, and it seemed like Satan was surrounding me with parents boasting about their son's prom or graduation. All I could do was smile and say, "Congratulations," while deep inside I was wishing it had been my son as well. I shed a few tears, but I also trusted God's guidance that my son and I were exactly where the Lord wanted us to be. Months later, after a Sunday service, while serving in the children's ministry, I heard this loud "Momma" and before I could look, huge arms were holding me so tight. We both stood in the church lobby, holding each other and crying. I was so stunned. My first question was, "How did you find me?" and it felt good hearing him say "where else would you be on a Sunday but in church and in children's ministry." It had been almost five years since we'd seen each other or been in contact.

We're now living in a pandemic, and my son didn't graduate from high school; however, he did get his GED on his own, with some encouragement from Momma. I was later honored to attend his graduation for his certification to teach children with the same special needs he had. Ironically, his students are children with issues in anger management, separation anxiety, disobedience, rebellion, etc., but who better to understand these children than one who has actually experienced the same issues. My son has aged out of the system and has his own apartment where he lives by himself, paying his own bills, and caring for his own needs. He once said to me, "Momma, working and making a living is hard stuff." I smiled and said, "Welcome to the world of becoming a man." My son still has a long way to go to become a man, but I am so proud of how far he has come. We committed to having lengthy conversations and respect for each other. He has apologized in so many ways, not just in word, and I can tell that he has been praying. Our relationship is still mending, and he knows that it will take some time—years—before the trust is there again. However, the first step was forgiveness which has been accomplished. Reconciliation has been established, and the relationship is mending. We have gone to church together on several occasions.

My son shared with me how challenging it was for him being back in the system. He states he was moved to and from multiple group homes and admits it was mainly due to his behavior. However, he came to a point where he didn't care anymore. It was a few good men, one being a world changer from my church, who didn't know me nor I him, but I recently learned that it was his imparting of wisdom to my son that made a difference. Isaiah had to overcome many obstacles and hardships and learn lessons through the "school of hard knocks" as the old folks say, but he did learn. God is a master planner, and He caused all things to work together for good. Thanks be to God who redeemed my son from the error of his ways and the evil that was stalking him. I don't think there could have been any other way.

EPILOGUE

Adoption is the most selfless act anyone could ever do. The giving of oneself requires love, patience, time, perseverance, and stamina, just to name a few. These are the same requirements needed for any biological parent. I have no regrets whatsoever regarding the adoption of my son. However, I would have never made it without the guidance of the Holy Spirit. I am so blessed to have been led to a church where the pastor teaches the word of God with understanding in a way to use it in daily life. Although there is training available for those who want to adopt, there is nothing that will prepare you for parenting an adopted child, especially one with special needs. There is *no training* that will prepare you for the partnership required to adopt from and through the Department of Family and Children Services. Therefore, when you don't know what to do, you need the Lord to guide you.

I have grown in so many ways as a result of my son's adoption. I've learned just as much from my son as he has from me. Ironically, the thing I had feared the most was losing my son, and that fear came upon me (just like Job). Once that fear was dealt with by my rebuking the fear and letting go, God was able to do his great works in both my son and me. In hindsight, I realize that fear was crippling my relationship with my son—fear of being judged wrong, fear of DFCS, fear of being jailed, fear of making the wrong decisions, fear of being a bad parent, fear of my son being mistreated, fear of what people would say, fear of what my family would say, fear of failure, and more fear. *The Devil is a liar!* I had to accept the fact that God loves me, and God loves Isaiah, and because of this, we have nothing to fear because *love* gets rid of fear, and adoption is one of the greatest act of love!

I wish I could provide you with an understanding of why I had to go through all the experiences I went through during the raising of my son. The hours of standing in the heat of the sun for a box of canned goods, the hours of standing in the rain for help to pay just one bill, and hours of sitting in the welfare office for food stamps, only to be denied. So much time was wasted in waiting for a little bit of a handout, which would never be the answer, but was very much needed at the time. I couldn't believe the fact that I was a professional woman with a degree and a license, yet I was made to bow to a system of corruption and contempt for the sake of my son's well-being. It was important to me that he had food to eat, clothes on his back, and a roof over his head—a roof with running warm water, electricity, and heat. I wish I could explain my sitting in a jail cell on a cold metal bench for hours for doing absolutely nothing except giving my heart to a child in need. I wish I could explain the *years* of being tormented by the court after clearance from DFCS and CPS for their errors. I don't understand why, for a minute in time, I had lost my freedom, my standards of living, my job, my home, my son, all starting with a Caucasian teacher who thought she was doing something heroic by calling DFCS to report a bruise on the wrist.

I'm sure there are some who will say that I went through all the hell because I shouldn't have adopted in the first place, or maybe because I've sinned. However, since we *all* sin, this obviously can't be the answer. As for the former, I know what the voice of God sounds like, and I'm convinced that the decision to adopt was His doing, evidenced by my victory in every situation and every circumstance I had to face. I'm still standing. God provides mercy and grace, even with mistakes. This is true, however I don't believe God needs to put someone through hell for a mistake, especially since Jesus has already been to hell for me. So let's go back to the beginning where I stated my definition of DFACS: Demonic Forces Against Children's Spirits.

The enemy is so fearful of our children; after all, they are the future! I believe with all my heart that the system called DFCS is spiritually owned and operated by it's CEO, whose name is Satan. To be clear, I'm not saying that the people who work at DFCS are demonic, possessed, or anything like that, however, the *system* is so corrupt and dysfunctional, only an overhaul could repair it, but who is able, capable, or wise enough for the correction of such a massive, statewide system? For years, the system has operated on an imbalanced of money being funneled in to what *looks like* profitable and beneficial resources. Remember, the CEO is the father of lies and excellent at deception; he even fooled Mother Eve several years ago, right in front of her spouse, Adam.

It appears too easy to leave an abandoned child in a system that is already overwhelmed with children and limited in help and support, a system that is already dysfunctional due to red tape beauracracy and limited wisdom. As of 2022, a person can leave a child on the step of a fire department or police department without any consequence of action, and that child will become a state responsibility, our responsibility indirectly. To add insult to injury, there is no collaboration between DFCS, CPS, and the local police department, which is an outrage! One would think that the law would at least be on the same page, but this is not the case at all as evidenced by my own experience. I personally call the system "The Beast."

I believe my challenges were meant to help people facing similar situations whether it's now or in the future. This book is meant to be a blessing to whoever will embrace the miracle of adoption and stick with it long enough to watch it unfold. I hope it will awaken the children of light to reach out to these children in need of love and awaken society to this massive monster devouring children, called Department of Family and Children Services.

I encourage anyone and everyone who is able and has the means to do so to adopt. There are plenty of children waiting to be loved. However, I strongly recommend you pray about it and do your research. Hopefully, my experiences will help kick-start you in the right direction to seek the answers you need. By no means am I an expert on adoption. I'm just a parent who has been there and done it as a single parent. It's important as a parent to have a good strong foundation in the Word of God. My faith was the glue that held my son and me together through the trials and tribulations of life. Because I provided him with a Word-based foundation at a very young age, it carried him through the years he was away from me. Train up a child in the way he should go, and when he is old enough, he will not depart from it (Proverbs).

My son continues to develop into the man God created him to be. I continue to develop into the woman God created me to be. I have done all I could as his mother, and now Isaiah is the key person on his own journey in life. I thank God that so far, Isaiah has never been hooked on drugs or in jail as he has a strong foundation in the Word of God. I missed my son graduating from high school, but I was blessed to see him graduate for his teacher's certification. My son is a blessing to me and to all the students he's now touching with his love and the Word. Ironically, he is teaching children, some who have the same emotional behavior issues as he once had. It was the love of God and the Word of God which tamed his anger issues and rebellion. To watch him work with these children with needs is absolutely amazing!

We are still working on our mother-son relationship, and we are still growing. However, he had to go through hell and back to learn the lessons God has for him. Isaiah recently told me that my releasing him back in to the system turned out to be a blessing because even though it was a hard lesson for him to learn, it made him grow up. He admitted taking my love and his freedom for granted. Having to go from group home to group home made him realize the luxury he really had. He realized the importance for morals and values and overall good conduct. I had to learn that it wasn't enough to just love him and hold onto him; I had to love him yet provide him with something more by letting him go. It's called tough love because this is what you do *when love is not enough.*

It is finished.